NO ONE ELSE
I'D RATHER BE

No One Else I'd Rather Be

Loving a Daughter with ADHD for Who She Is

A Memoir

Aimee Kaufman

SHE WRITES PRESS

Published 2025
Printed in the United States of America
Print ISBN: 978-1-64742-828-0
E-ISBN: 978-1-64742-829-7
Library of Congress Control Number: 2024915596

For information, address:
She Writes Press
1569 Solano Ave #546
Berkeley, CA 94707

Interior Design by Kiran Spees

She Writes Press is a division of SparkPoint Studio, LLC.

CONTENTS

PREFACE

Dear Dr. Rosen,

A few things you have said to me during our sessions have stuck in my mind and made me think long and hard about my daughter Samantha (Sam) and my role in her development. One is that I shouldn't use Attention Deficit Hyperactivity Disorder (ADHD) as an excuse for her inappropriate behavior. Two is that you think I created a "monster."

I want to explain to you why I believe that many of Sam's actions and inappropriate behaviors are inherent to her disability. I do not believe, as you have professed, that this was created by my inability to discipline or control her.

Ever since Sam was a toddler, she has been a difficult child to figure out. At first, I thought her temper tantrums and defiant behavior were due to the "terrible twos" syndrome. Early on, I reached out to a therapist who diagnosed the problem, without meeting Sam or her older sister Dana, as sibling rivalry . . . When Sam would not respond to traditional discipline, I reached out to other therapists and school administrators. I tried many of their recommendations and continually asked if they thought she had ADHD. The answer was always no . . . In hopes of finding a conclusive diagnosis, we had Sam tested in fourth grade . . . The doctor determined that she did not have ADHD . . . Sam's fifth-grade teacher began to notice problems in the classroom and suggested that we have her tested again . . . Without a doubt, this doctor diagnosed Sam with ADHD. That's when we started her on Ritalin. We saw a dramatic, positive change in her behavior. We were so pleased to see that something finally worked. All of the discipline, punishments, and attempts at finding help for Sam had previously failed until we put her on Ritalin.

Since fifth grade, Sam's behavior has definitely improved . . . Our house quieted down, and we seemed to have had more good days than bad . . . Sam's problems were more manageable until eighth grade when she started saying that she hated herself and wished she were dead. As you know, that's when we found you.

So, here we are a year later. Sam's in ninth grade, and her behavior is worse than ever. We are at our wit's end. As you pointed out, we do not have control over Sam. You are absolutely correct. She doesn't respond to authority, discipline, or punishment. However, I refuse to believe it's because I haven't tried to control or discipline her . . . I believe that the "monster" (you claim I helped create) is the result of a biological disability. I also believe that Ritalin and my unconditional love and compassion for Sam have temporarily tamed the "monster" throughout her life. It is obvious from the history I presented in this letter that my attempts at trying to help Sam change her behavior haven't worked. I can't help but believe that ADHD **is** a valid excuse. Maybe Ritalin is not as effective as it used to be, and maybe Sam will always have a hard time controlling the symptoms of her "disability."

It seems to me that because of ADHD, Sam does not have the internal mechanisms to control her emotions and reactions to conflicts in her life. Instead of trying to change Sam to react differently, I think we should be trying to identify the source of her conflicts and help her eliminate them. My guess is that positive behavior will follow. Not because my husband, Barry, our older daughter, Dana, and I stand up to her, as you have suggested, but because we help her settle internal conflicts. We have been focusing on the outrageous behavior instead *of the source. Sam had mono this year, her grades have dropped, she is jealous of her older sister planning for college, and she is having problems with some of her teachers and friends. Maybe she is bossing us around to get attention. For Sam, negative attention may be better than none.*

I want you to know that I am writing this letter to help Sam, not to alleviate my own discomfort because you are blaming me for her problems. Things I have done in the past haven't worked in helping her find inner peace or self-control. Maybe, together, we can change directions and discover alternative ways to help Sam deal with her "disability."

Please let me know what you think,

Aimee

Rereading this letter I had written to Sam's therapist many years prior and transcribing excerpts into my memoir brought back feelings of anguish and frustration that are extremely painful to revisit. Although many disagreed, I always sensed that Sam could not control her outbursts and that her outrageous behavior was not my fault. Even though I often doubted myself, I refused to believe that Sam acted the way she did or that she was intentionally rude and disrespectful because of me. Trying to remain true to myself, I disregarded judgmental assessments and focused my intentions inward. Over time, I learned not to rely on those who, more often than not, offered misguided advice and hurtful accusations but instead on the one person I trusted the most to help me navigate the turbulent storms: me.

I read many books about ADHD that listed the symptoms, outlined diagnostic approaches, and discussed the pros and cons of available medications, behavior therapies, and alternative treatments, but typically, I was disappointed when I inevitably walked away from these self-help, reference-type books (with highlighter in hand) feeling overwhelmed, discouraged, and extremely helpless. Although

I learned a lot about ADHD, my approach to raising my troubled daughter—which focused on unconditional love and compassion as opposed to discipline, rules, and consequences—often seemed contradictory to some of the advice offered in those books. Thus, my search for answers typically remained unsatisfied, as the daily struggles of raising a child with ADHD continued to be a daunting and isolating task for me. Over time, I gained confidence in my own judgment and learned to follow my head and my heart instead of the recommendations presented in the books I read.

As Sam prepared to graduate from college, I found myself reflecting on her life. I marveled at how much she and I had overcome to reach that monumental milestone; it wasn't an easy accomplishment for either of us. With my emotions running high, I sat down at my computer and began to document the journey we'd taken over the course of the previous twenty-two years.

Recognizing that my transcribing the troubling memories of our family's past might be painful for Sam and for me, I initially considered keeping my very personal thoughts private. However, the more I wrote, the more I felt that what I was writing might be a source of comfort to other parents who are struggling with similar issues. With this in mind, I talked to Sam, and when she gave me consent to move forward, I decided to turn my reflections into a memoir. Putting aside my own uneasiness, I began to formulate my ideas about a different kind of book—one written for the average mom like me, one I wished had been available to me when I was feeling overwhelmingly defeated and inadequate at the job of motherhood.

Throughout the many years of my own uncertainty and insecurity, I often longed for someone who could relate to my daunting experiences of parenting a child with ADHD and who could have helped me believe that there might be a bright light at the end of my dark tunnel. Someone who could validate my feelings and provide a shoulder to lean on when my daughter's erratic behavior became so severe that our family dynamics suffered. Someone to rely on, not only when I was feeling overwhelmed by the constant attention Sam demanded of me but also during the many times I spent throughout her childhood tackling conflicts with her teachers, therapists, and doctors, tolerating hurtful criticism from family members and friends, and agonizing over the never-ending decisions about ADHD medications.

Since my longing was never satisfied, I hope, through telling my story, to be that person for other parents who are wrestling with similar challenges as they raise a child with ADHD and are feeling the same humiliation, isolation, and self-doubt that I experienced while seeking help from those who often criticized my parenting abilities and blamed me for my daughter's problems. I want them to know that they are not alone in their search for answers, to remind them to trust their instincts, and, most importantly, to encourage them to never give up hope that they will one day find the bright light at the end of their own dark tunnel.

I also wrote this book for all of the children out there with ADHD and the teachers, therapists, doctors, camp counselors, extended family members, and others in their orbit. It would warm my heart if our family's story could help prevent other children from feeling the same embarrassment, self-doubt, frustration, and inferiority that Sam experienced while in the care of those who lacked the knowledge needed to help children with ADHD succeed and feel good about themselves.

I realize how fortunate Sam and I are that our relationship remained intact throughout the difficult years. By never losing sight of our deep love for each other—by not letting ADHD get in our way—we grew closer. Sam's ability to succeed academically, to thrive in her career, and to develop a relationship with a wonderful person who wants to spend the rest of his life with her is a testament to her strong character and drive to be the best version of herself for all to see. When I think of the innumerable challenges our family over-came to get to this moment, I can't help but smile from a place deep inside my heart.

INTRODUCTION

IT'S NOT EASY BEING ME (OR SAM)

SAM CLIMBED INTO MY MITSUBISHI Montero after dance class, clearly lost in her thoughts, with a pensive expression on her face. Worried by the change in her demeanor from earlier in the day when she happily sang along to her favorite song on the radio, I opened my mouth to ask her what was wrong.

Before I had a chance to say a word, Sam turned to me with a pained look in her eyes and declared, "It's not easy being me!"

It took me a few moments to process what she had just said and how I was going to respond. Sam often told me that she didn't know why she acted the way she did when she lost control of her emotions, and she regretted saying mean things to me and others, but it wasn't until this moment that I fully understood the extent of the stress she was experiencing.

With a heavy heart, I tried to ease Sam's distress. "Oh, Sammy, I understand how you must be feeling. I'm proud of you for telling me. I promise we are going to find someone to help. And I promise I won't give up. Until then, know how much I love you and I'm here for you always." I didn't know what my next steps would be. But for my Sam, I was willing to do whatever it took.

~

Sitting alone in the psychiatrist's office, waiting for the results of an extensive psychiatric evaluation of my daughter—my heart racing and my hands sweating—was agonizing.

Finally, the doctor walked in. She sat down at her desk, looked up from her file, and unequivocally announced, "Of course—Sam has ADHD!"

Before I could ask any of my many questions, I was overcome with emotion. My voice escaped me as tears rolled down my cheeks.

With a confused look on her face, the psychiatrist asked, "Mrs. Kaufman, are you okay?"

Of course, I'm not okay! I wanted to scream. *I can't be the only mother who has cried in your office after hearing her daughter has ADHD. Or am I?* Instead of blurting out my thoughts, I took a moment to gain my composure, dried my eyes, took a deep breath, and tried to explain myself.

"After years of searching for answers, I'm relieved to finally have the name of a disability to attribute to Sam's behavior," I told her in a shaky voice. Holding back more tears, I admitted, "But I'm also extremely overwhelmed. I need time to process this new revelation."

Prior to that moment, when Sam was ten years old, I'd often questioned whether or not her out-of-control behavior had something to do with my style of parenting. Since I was often criticized by many people who believed that her problems stemmed from the fact that I wasn't strict enough and that I didn't discipline her correctly, how could I not feel some responsibility? But each time I locked myself in the bathroom after a heated argument with Sam, I couldn't help but believe that her problems were extremely complex and that she needed a lot more than me simply changing my parenting techniques. Since recommendations from others failed to provide positive results, I learned to follow my maternal instincts and continued to raise Sam the only way I knew how—with love, compassion, and understanding. The same way my mother raised me.

It wasn't until that day that I finally discovered the reason behind her outrageous behavior, inability to focus, and nonexistent self-control. So yes, I cried, not because of the implications of the diagnosis but because I finally had the answer to why my daughter acted the way she did—and because I finally believed that it wasn't my fault!

ADHD is a disability that affects an entire family, not just the person diagnosed with it. It becomes a true test of a parent's unconditional love and, in our family, a sister's adoration and devotion to her often-disruptive sibling. Dealing with ADHD can be a lifelong struggle for the person living with the disability and a roller coaster ride for those directly in their path. Sam's words, "It's not easy being me," not only expressed her feelings about her life as she suffered from the symptoms of ADHD and the side effects of her medications, but they also echoed what everyone in our immediate family felt as we struggled with the reverberations Sam's ADHD sent through our lives.

In the pages to come, I will highlight how painful it was for me as I wrestled with the uncertainties of raising a defiant yet loving child with ADHD. And how, in spite of the daily conflicts and uncharted challenges, I continued to love my daughter with all my heart and all my soul and trust that underneath her combative exterior, Sam continued to feel the same way about me. This mutual love is the one thing that Sam and I always counted on when things got out of control, and what, I believe, saved our family from falling apart during the toughest times.

It's also what I believe helped Sam evolve from the tormented girl she was that day after dance class to the person who would eventually say—many years later, as she was coming into her own as a young adult— "There's no one else I'd rather be."

1

LET'S START AT THE VERY BEGINNING

WHEN A MOTHER IS PREPARING to have a second child, it's not unusual for her to expect the parenting experience to be similar to that of the first. After all, with the exact same parents, how different can two children really be?

That's exactly what I thought when I got pregnant for a second time.

My older daughter, Dana, was born with an easygoing personality and a strong desire to please. Twenty-six months later, I gave birth to Sam with high hopes for a repeat performance. From the moment I held my newborn in my arms, however, I realized how unrealistic my expectations were. As we cuddled in bed at the hospital those first few days and I fell in love with the newest addition to our family, a protective feeling came over me. I wondered how Sam would fare following in Dana's footsteps and suspected that her path might not be easy. Somehow, I knew from the beginning that Sam was going to march to the beat of a different drum and that living up to the high standards already set by her older sister might be a challenge. As she grew older and her personality began to emerge, I quickly learned that two children born to the exact same parents can be extreme opposites in many respects—even to the point that one might wonder if there was a mix-up at the hospital!

One of my earliest entries in Sam's baby book tells a different story, however:

Sam is a very happy baby. At 2 ½ weeks, she started sleeping through the night. Sam smiles a lot. She watches her mobile and Dana! Sam takes long naps.

What surprised me the most as I read through this journal years later was that I had forgotten how tranquil Sam was upon her arrival home from the hospital—how well she slept, how easy she was to care for. At one point, I checked the cover to make sure I wasn't reading Dana's book by mistake.

Apparently, the change in her demeanor that shortly followed clouded my memory. I wish I had referred to those pages more often during the years that followed to remind myself that Sam entered the world as a happy, content baby girl. Remembering those peaceful times might have provided comfort along the way—and hope for the future.

Driving home after dropping Dana at preschool one day—me in my pajamas and Sam, who was a few months old, strapped into her car seat—I turned on my favorite Springsteen song and planned out my morning activities. *Put Sam down for a nap. Take a nice hot shower. Put on my makeup. Dry my hair. Get dressed. Prepare Sam's bottle and wait for her to wake up.* Sounded like a good plan to me!

When we arrived home, I jumped into action. Expecting her to sleep for an hour or two, as she usually did, I put Sam into her crib and tiptoed out of the room, taking the intercom with me. Step one accomplished!

I walked down the hall to my bedroom, placed the intercom on the bathroom vanity, and turned on the shower. While the water was getting hot, I picked out my clothes. When steam started seeping into the bedroom, I removed my pajamas, hopped into the shower, and savored the feeling of the water running through my hair. *Ahhhhh!* Step two accomplished!

But seconds later, through the sound of the water splashing onto the tile, I heard crying coming from the intercom.

Noooooo!! It's only been ten minutes since I put you down!

With Sam's sobbing getting louder and more persistent, I quickly washed, turned off the shower, and threw on a robe, then ran into Sam's room and tried to lull her back to sleep. No luck with that! Sam kept screaming, so I picked her up and placed her in the newly assembled baby swing in my bathroom while I attempted to dry my hair and finish getting dressed—but no luck with that either. Unlike Dana, who had always been happy in her swing, Sam wanted out and into my arms.

Just like that, my happy, content baby girl had changed her sleeping pattern and became an infant who was easily distressed. I tried not to worry too much. *It's probably just an isolated incident*, I assured myself.

As the weeks passed, however, I found it challenging to attend to the needs of both children. Sam was growing more and more demanding of my attention, and she was no longer able to entertain herself with a mobile or other age-appropriate toys like her older sister often did. Although I hoped it wasn't true, I worried that the days of getting to take a shower, dry my hair, put on my makeup, and get dressed one right after the other were gone for good.

As hard as it was for me to keep my composure and properly care for the girls during the day, I dreaded the hours between five and seven in the evening the most. For one reason or another, someone was typically crying, and often, that someone was me.

My husband, Barry, an attorney who worked late most nights, wasn't available to participate in most of our early evening activities, which meant I was often on my own.

One night, as I was sitting at the kitchen table holding Sam in the crook of my arm, giving her a bottle with one hand while I was trying to feed Dana with the other, the phone rang. Annoyed with the intrusion, I rolled my eyes. *Really? Don't people know they should never call a house with two young children at dinnertime?*

Somehow, I managed to jockey the kids, the bottle, and the spoon so I could answer. Trying to hide my annoyance—but probably failing—I said, "Hello?"

"Hi Aim, how's it going?"

As soon as I heard Barry's sheepish voice on the other end of the line, I began to cry. I was expecting him to be on his way home, but upon looking at the caller ID, I realized he was still at his office, which meant he wouldn't be home for at least another hour.

When I didn't answer right away—Sam had started to cry when I stopped feeding her, and Dana had grabbed the knife I'd left on the table after cutting her food, so I was a little preoccupied—he continued, "I'm really sorry, but my meeting is running late so I haven't left the office yet."

I sighed into the phone, revealing my disappointment. "Again? This is the second time this week." I didn't wait for him to respond. "Whatever," I snapped. "I need to hang up and deal with the kids."

It wasn't the first time this happened, and, unfortunately, it wouldn't be the last.

Nothing could have prepared me for the feelings of inadequacy that came over me after Sam's birth. Prior to having children, I worked full time as a CPA in a large public accounting firm. I was used to hard work and long hours. When Dana was born, I knew that I wanted to be a hands-on mom, so returning to a full-time job was out of the question for me.

I wasn't, however, ready to be a full-time homemaker, either, so I hired a woman to care for Dana a few days a week while I worked part-time as a tax research analyst for a private corporation. It was a decision that curtailed my professional opportunities and jeopardized my chances of one day becoming a partner in a CPA firm, but it was a decision I never once regretted. I let my heart—which had never let me down thus far—guide me in a direction that felt perfectly right for me and my family. With my new work schedule in place, I was able to juggle my redefined profession and care for Dana without doubting my parenting abilities or feeling inadequate.

Jump ahead twenty-six months to when Sam entered the picture, and I found myself struggling. Questions continually invaded my thoughts as I wondered why that was the case. *Why can't I handle the added responsibility without feeling so overwhelmed? Why is Sam such a difficult child to figure out? What am I doing wrong?*

These questions persisted throughout my maternity leave, and as it approached the end, I sat my insecure self down and weighed my options. Did I have enough confidence to return to my job and become a working mother of two, or should I give in to my fears and become a stay-at-home mom? My internal debate went from *No way can you handle working and parenting Dana and my Velcro-child Sam* to *Of course, you can handle the added responsibility. Sam is probably just going through a difficult stage. You're stronger than you think.*

As I made my final decision, I took into consideration the advice of the college professors who had encouraged me to pursue a career in a field that was dominated by men. As a result of their support back then, and my strong desire to succeed, I became a CPA and excelled in my field. Just as important, I enjoyed the work I performed. Taking all of this into consideration, I came to the conclusion that I wasn't ready to give that up.

You can do this, Aimee! I urged myself during a silent but enthusiastic pep talk. Thus, self-encouraged, I put aside my uncertainties and mustered up the courage to head back to my part-time job.

2

WANTED . . . A NANNY FOR TWO ADORABLE CHILDREN

I TRIED TO CALM MY NERVES as I dialed the number. Hiring a live-in nanny was a big deal.

Now that I was officially returning to my job when my maternity leave ended, Barry and I had discussed our childcare options. In light of my own trepidations and Barry's demanding work schedule, we'd decided that hiring a live-in caretaker was the way to go. But finding the perfect nanny—with *Mary Poppins* in the back of my mind—was not as easy as I had anticipated. I'd scoured the newspapers and called numerous agencies before finally finding a woman from the Midwest who, on the surface, appeared to be ideal for our family. Feeling optimistic, I arranged a telephone interview, and now the appointed time had arrived.

I was extremely nervous, to say the least. When I heard the soft, kind voice on the other end of the line, however, I regained my composure and jumped right in.

"Hi Trixie, this is Aimee. As you know from the agency, I'm looking to hire a nanny for my two girls." After telling her about Dana and Sam and filling her in on the logistics of the job, I asked her to tell me about her experiences.

"Well," Trixie began, "I've taken care of young children in my hometown, and I am currently working as a janitor in a school to supplement my income. I am willing to relocate to New Jersey with my car and take on a job as a live-in nanny. If you like, I can send you references."

"That would be wonderful," I said.

We chatted for a few more minutes, then ended the call. I hung up the phone feeling optimistic. When I saw the positive reviews from previous employers she sent to me later that day, I made my decision almost immediately. I was still apprehensive about having a stranger living in our house, of course, but she had sounded really nice on the phone, and she had experience taking care of young children.

The following day, I took a leap of faith and called her back. "Hi, Trixie, this is Aimee again. I was excited to hear all of the positive feedback from your previous employers, so I want to offer you the job and ask you to drive cross-country to be our nanny. I hope you are still interested."

"Hi, Aimee. Thanks for calling back!" she said. "Yes, I am still interested. I need to tie up a few loose ends here, so how about I get to you in a week? I hope that works for you."

"That would be great," I replied.

After we went over a few logistics, I hung up the phone with a smile on my face. Relieved that my search was over, I went to tell Dana and Sam . . . even though Sam was too young to understand!

"Dana, can you help me get the house organized before Trixie gets here?" It was the day of our new nanny's arrival, and I wanted to make a good first impression. I'd woken the girls early, and Dana had been working diligently since breakfast, putting her toys away and tossing her clothes into the hamper while I'd been at work cleaning the bathrooms and putting new sheets on the bed in our spare room. I was pleased to see that Sam was happy in her playpen, enjoying the music I had turned on for her. When there was nothing left to clean, I sat Dana and Sam in front of the TV and turned on our *Mary Poppins* video to watch while we waited for this new stage in our lives to begin.

When the doorbell rang, Dana ran to answer while—excited and nervous at the same time—I picked up Sam and followed behind.

When I opened the door, Dana chimed right in, "Hi, I'm Dana, and this is my baby sister Sam. Do you want to play a game with me? Or watch a video?"

Noticing disappointment on Dana's face when there was no response, I jumped in and greeted our new nanny. "Welcome to New Jersey, Trixie! I'm Aimee. It looks like you've already met Dana—and this is Sam." I tickled Sam and got a smile out of her since I wanted her to make a good first impression also. "Why don't I help you bring your things in from the car and get you settled into your room?"

In a quiet, meek voice, looking down at the ground, Trixie replied, "Okay, that sounds fine."

I put Sam back in her playpen and went outside. I felt uneasy as I helped Trixie unpack her car. We seemed to be off to an awkward beginning, though I wasn't quite sure why. Disheartened, I started questioning my decision. My first impression of our new nanny was that she was quite guarded. I was disappointed to not feel an immediate connection. I sensed that this person, the person who was going to be living in our house, was shy and uncomfortable in her new surroundings. She had a hard time looking me in the eye or engaging in conversation with me or the children. Hoping my instincts would be proven wrong as time passed, I pushed aside my apprehension and did what I could to help the girls—and myself—acclimate to their new caretaker.

I dragged my feet as I got dressed. It was my first day back to work, and I was nervous about leaving Dana and Sam with Trixie. Given our uncomfortable meeting and continued awkwardness, I wasn't sure if I was prepared to entrust my daughters to her care. When it was time for me to leave, I took my time walking down the stairs so I could hear what was going on in the kitchen. As usual, Dana was chatting away, and Sam was babbling back to her. I was pleased to see that everything seemed to be under control.

Breathing a sigh of relief, I stepped into the kitchen and said, "Okay, girls, it's time for mommy to head out."

Dana stopped talking mid-sentence, ran to give me a hug and kiss, and then continued telling her story to Sam and the new member of her audience.

Still feeling a bit uneasy, I walked over to Sam's highchair, gave her a hug and kiss, and said, "Goodbye, girls! Have a fun day!"

I walked down the stairs to the front hall very slowly, waiting to see if anyone was going to cry or complain that I was leaving. When that didn't happen, I opened the door and closed it behind me with a smile on my face. I was feeling good as I got into my car and drove away. I was excited to be going back to work and hopeful that things were going to be just fine at home.

I was entertaining our guests when I heard Sam crying. Shortly after, Trixie entered the kitchen. "I just put Sam into your sister's lap so I could come help you," she explained with a shrug.

Trixie had been with us for a few months now, and I was happy to see the girls responding well to our new situation. But recently, I had noticed some worrisome changes in Sam. The most troubling to me was that she'd been consistently rejecting family members, including me, in favor of Trixie. And now here she was, at a holiday gathering in our house, doing it again.

My sister tried to calm Sam down by distracting her. "It's okay, Sammy. Aunt Cindy is going to read your favorite book to you." But Sam wanted nothing to do with her aunt and continued crying.

My mother tried next. Grandma Glady loved playing Clap Hands with Sam, so she got down on the floor and started to sing. "Clap hands, clap hands 'til daddy comes home . . ."

No matter what they tried, Sam just wouldn't engage. She continued to cry until she saw Trixie heading back to the living room to hold her.

Our relatives weren't the only ones getting the cold shoulder from Sam. I also noticed that she was rejecting *me* at times. I was always excited to see the girls when I got home from work, but the reception I'd been receiving from Sam lately was not always a positive one.

I tried not to take it to heart when Sam acted out upon my return. I convinced myself that this type of behavior was typical for children of working mothers—even though Dana never acted that way. I was so determined for everything to be fine that I ignored the early signs that maybe something wasn't quite right with our caretaker situation.

One day, as I was walking downstairs from my bedroom, I noticed Dana off by herself in the living room while Trixie was playing with Sam on the couch. Before anyone saw me, I heard Dana ask, "Can I play with you and Sammy?"

I was surprised when I heard the reply: "Sorry, Dana. This is a baby's game. Why don't you go downstairs and watch a video?"

I poked my head into the room and saw that Dana looked like she was going to cry. Wanting to cheer her up, I went into the kitchen and called out to her, "Hey Danes, I could use some help. Why don't you come set the table and pick out what you want to drink?"

She perked right up and came to help me. But the interaction didn't sit well with me at all. I resolved to keep a closer eye on things.

The more I saw, the stronger my concerns grew, especially on the day I took Trixie and Sam to see Dana in a pre-school performance. Trixie sat on the floor of the classroom with Sam in her lap while I took a video of Dana singing and dancing. Of course, I thought Dana was adorable, but when it was over, I asked Trixie, "So, how did you like the show?"

"Oh, well, I was keeping Sam occupied, so I didn't see much," she said sheepishly, without looking up.

I was glad Sam liked her so much, but I was disappointed at Trixie's blatant lack of interest in Dana. She was supposed to be a nanny to *both* our girls, not just Sam. Dana was four now, and she needed affection and attention too. Were those needs being neglected?

"Baby girl, please come sit with me for a few minutes," I said to Dana one morning, patting the bed next to me. "I want to ask you a few questions." Thinking that I might be overreacting, I decided to ask Dana how she felt about the situation before I made any decisions.

She sat down with an inquisitive look on her face. "About what, Mommy?"

"Can you tell me how you feel about Trixie and the things you do together?"

"Well, I don't think she likes me very much," Dana said sadly. "She treats me much differently than Sammy. Yesterday, she made me sit in the corner when I told her I didn't want to watch a TV show she was putting on for Sam. I didn't know what I did wrong, so I cried. She didn't come over to me or ask why I was upset. She never tries to play with me or asks me what I want to watch."

Learning how upset and confused Dana was confirmed my suspicion that Trixie was favoring Sam over Dana. This unsettling feeling that had been hiding deep down in my gut erupted and dominated my thoughts. It wasn't just Sam's growing rejection of family members—including me—or Dana's hurt feelings. I had also noticed Sam's demeanor changing, and not for the better, during Trixie's time with us. Temper tantrums and impatience often replaced the contentment and tranquility of her early days.

Taking into consideration Dana's input and my observations, I concluded that this relationship was negatively affecting our family dynamics—and it was time to make a change.

On the day of Trixie's departure, when Sam was two-and-a-half years old and Dana four-and-a-half, my instincts and Dana's hurt feelings were validated by the source of my worries. During our awkward goodbyes, I was taken aback when she started to speak first.

"I want you to know that I resented you leaving Sam home with me while you would take Dana on special outings with your friends and their children," she blurted out. "From what I could see, you favored Dana over Sam, so I did the opposite. I paid more attention to Sam rather than Dana."

Although I didn't feel that I owed her an explanation for how I chose to raise my children, her disapproval angered me. I'm sure my voice sounded defensive as I replied, "Look, I chose to hire a nanny not only so I could go back to work but to have someone I trusted to care for my baby while I continued to do age-appropriate things with Dana. I made this decision to help Dana through the transition, in hopes of avoiding any resentment toward her sister. And keep in mind, I left Dana home with you at times when I would take Sam to Baby Power classes or other age-appropriate events. For Dana's sake, it's unfortunate that you didn't understand this."

She was seemingly unmoved by what I had said and didn't respond. Before she walked out of the door, however, she added one more thing that raised my antennae and caught me completely off guard. "And I think part of the reason why I didn't feel comfortable here is that your Jewish background is so different than my Mormon upbringing."

Given the fact that we weren't observant Jews (we didn't even belong to a temple at the time), I thought this was strange. I wondered if she had some anti-Semitic views. This comment only convinced me further that I was making the right decision by letting her go.

Without further discussion, we said our goodbyes, she drove off, and I closed the door in disbelief.

I was upset to have learned all of this much later than I would have liked, and I'm embarrassed to admit that it took me almost two years from the time Trixie arrived to come to the realization that Sam's rejection of our family members was more likely a direct result of Trixie's favoritism toward her. I hesitated to blame the nanny for Sam's changed behavior, but at the time—and not knowing about ADHD—I couldn't help but wonder.

3

JUST A SPOONFUL OF SUGAR

"HELLO, MRS. KAUFMAN. This is Diane from Sundance School. I'm calling to let you know that the principal would like to meet with you this afternoon. He is wondering if you can stop by for a few minutes before class is dismissed."

My heart started beating a little faster. Now that Sam was at school, being summoned to the principal's office wasn't always good news.

"Yes, that would be fine," I said hesitantly. "Can you tell me why he wants to meet with me?"

"I'm sorry, he didn't tell me what this was about," she said. "But should I let him know to expect you later this afternoon?"

"Yes, definitely," I replied, my mouth a little dry. "Thank you for calling."

For the rest of the afternoon, I watched the clock and counted the minutes until it was time to leave for the meeting. During the car ride, I couldn't stop worrying if this had something to do with Sam. *Did she talk back to her teacher again? Did she have a fight with a child in her class?*

Luckily, the school was only fifteen minutes from our house, so I didn't have much time to hypothesize about what I might be walking into when I arrived. Before I had a chance to allow my nerves to take over, I was parking my car and walking toward the school's entrance. I didn't have long to wait when I got to the principal's office, either—he saw me right away and waved me inside.

"Hello, Mrs. Kaufman. Thank you for coming in," he began. "I wanted to let you know that I recently heard about someone who is looking for work as a nanny."

I had totally forgotten that I had informed the preschool administrators that I was looking for a new nanny. My apprehension immediately started to dissipate.

As disillusioned as I was at the end of our first nanny experience, I hadn't given up hope that we would one day find our Mary Poppins. Since Trixie's departure, I'd been calling local agencies, placing ads in various newspapers, and asking everyone I came in contact with if they knew of anyone looking for a nanny position—with no luck. My hopes were dwindling, and my spirits were low as all of my efforts seemed to be failing.

Suddenly optimistic, I said, "Please tell me. Yes, I am definitely still looking for a replacement for the nanny who recently left."

"Well," he said, "there's a girl from England who had come to America to fill a previously arranged nanny job, but the position fell through after she arrived, leaving her without employment or a place to live. She is temporarily staying with another Sundance family until she finds a job. To make a long story short, I wanted to know if you are interested in meeting her."

Trying to contain my excitement, especially when I heard she was from England, I said, "Yes, of course," and dug into my pocketbook for a pen to take down her name and phone number.

After leaving the principal's office, I crossed my fingers and ran to get the girls from their classrooms. The minute I got home, I dialed the number, spoke to the woman whose house she was staying at, and set up an appointment for later that day.

∿

The doorbell rang right at the arranged time that afternoon. As I slowly opened the door, the girls peeking out from behind me, I took a deep breath and hoped for the best.

Liz jumped right in, wearing a radiant smile. "Hello, everyone. I'm Liz. I understand there are two little girls looking for a nanny!"

Much to my relief, my initial reaction was positive—I loved Liz's bubbly personality—so I pulled the girls out from behind me and introduced ourselves.

"Hi, Liz. I'm Aimee, and this is Dana and Sam, the two little girls you were asking about."

Without hesitation, Liz dropped to the floor and said in her endearing British accent, "Well, hello, Dana and Sam. It's so nice to meet you. Would you like to show me around the house? And maybe after, we can play a game. If that's okay with your mummy?"

The girls' heads swiveled in my direction with big smiles on their faces.

"Yes, of course," I replied with a big smile of my own.

As the girls ran off with Liz, I had a feeling we had finally found our Mary Poppins! An hour later, I joined the girls and Liz in Dana's room, where they were listening to music and playing a game. I was so moved by the immediate connection between my girls and Liz that I offered her the job on the spot.

Liz moved in the next day and was an absolute dream with Sam and Dana from the minute she arrived. She took them to the park and to visit friends in other towns. She sang silly songs with them and took them out for ice cream. She was constantly coming up with fun activities they could all do together. And, most important to me, she made a conscious effort to shower *both* girls with love and attention. Their bond was immediate and so deep that I almost couldn't believe our good luck.

Now that we had a nanny we trusted to care for the girls, Barry and I decided to celebrate our anniversary in Paradise Island. We hadn't traveled much since having children, so I was excited to be taking a vacation.

Prior to our departure, Sam, who was now three years old, developed upper respiratory congestion. We considered canceling altogether, but after taking her to the doctor and getting her medication, which seemed to be helping, we boarded the plane feeling confident that Liz could handle the next four days without us.

Everything was fine for the first three days, but on the last day of our trip, our confidence in our new nanny wavered for a moment when we received a terrifying phone call from my mother-in-law telling us that Sam was in the hospital.

We quickly learned that Liz had taken the girls to visit Barry's parents the night before. Shortly after their arrival, she noticed that Sam was having difficulty breathing. Luckily, Liz knew the signs of an asthma attack since she, too, suffered from the same debilitating disorder. Realizing Sam was in distress, she and my in-laws rushed her to the hospital. The doctors got Sam's breathing under control, but they insisted on keeping her overnight for observation. A frightened Sam had asked Liz to stay with her.

Reassured that Sam was okay, our faith in Liz was restored, but we were still eager to get home to our girls. We tried to put our worry aside as we waited anxiously for our flight to depart.

We rushed straight to the hospital after our plane landed that night. When we opened the door to the room, we found Liz sitting next to the crib with her back to us. Sam, who was attached to an IV and various monitors, was awake and noticed us first.

"Mommy, Daddy, you're here!" she cried out. "I missed you so much. I was so scared, but Lizzie stayed with me until you got back."

I immediately ran to Sam and gave her a big hug and lots of kisses.

I could tell she was exhausted, so I held her in my arms. Within minutes, she was fast asleep.

My heart ached to find my daughter in such a vulnerable state. Liz must have sensed my worry and stress because she quickly filled us in.

"Welcome home," she started. "I know you are worried about Sam, but the doctor said her condition is definitely improving. Since she refused to sleep until you got home, I sat with her throughout the night and all of today. I only left to go to the bathroom when Barry's parents came back to visit."

"Oh, Liz, I can't thank you enough," I said, tears in my eyes. "You must be exhausted. Why don't you go home now? We can talk more tomorrow." I reached out and gave her a big hug and lots of kisses as well—ones that said more than words could ever express. Then, I sent our devoted nanny home to get some well-deserved sleep.

Learning that Sam had chosen Liz to stay with her until we got home and that Liz had accepted the responsibility without hesitation, I knew in my heart that she had graduated from being our nanny to a cherished member of our family.

During the year Liz lived with us, I watched Sam and Dana flourish under her care. She adored both girls and learned how to deal with Sam's unruly conduct. Although Sam's defiant behavior continued to manifest, she began to reach out to others and develop loving relationships with her relatives. There's no doubt in my mind that Liz had a positive influence on Sam and on our entire family.

Everyone who knew Liz would surely agree that our very own Mary Poppins was kind, witty, sweet, and very pretty—and most importantly, she helped Sam accept her medication without a fuss! Similar to the children that Mary sang about in the song, "A Spoonful of Sugar."

4

WILL THE TERRIBLE TWOS EVER END?

I APPROACHED SAM'S BEDROOM ONE MORNING with a knot in my stomach. I had forgotten to do her laundry the night before. Sam's temper tantrums had intensified around the time she turned two years old—and maintained that intensity ever since. Typically, I had no idea what triggered her emotional outbursts, but getting dressed was a predictable downfall on any given day, especially during the stage in Sam's life when she insisted on wearing the same outfit for weeks in a row. Today, that outfit was too dirty for her to wear. Fearing the outburst that was sure to follow the disclosure of this news, I slowly turned the doorknob and walked in.

"Good morning, Sammy! It's time to wake up and get dressed for preschool!" I said, forcing a jovial tone. "Let's pick out your clothes, then go down and have breakfast."

As Sam climbed out of bed, she seemed to be in a good mood. "Hiiiii, Mommy," she cheerfully sang back at me. I already know what I want to wear. The blue skirt and my black shirt with a star on the front. The ones I wore yesterday."

Hoping to persuade her otherwise but already knowing that she wouldn't like my suggestion, I said, "Oh Sam, how about a different outfit since I didn't have time to wash those clothes last night? Why don't I help you pick something out?"

"Nooooo," she screamed. "I don't want to wear something else. I WANT TO WEAR THE BLUE SKIRT AND THE BLACK SHIRT!" She began to cry, and in between sobs, she yelled, "I hate you! You're the worst mother!"

As Sam's tirade escalated, my patience dwindled. She was going to be late for school if this argument kept going.

"Okay, okay!" I conceded. "Enough! Go get your skirt and shirt from the laundry basket, but I need you to stop crying and yelling at me. We can talk about this later and try to find other clothes you like to wear, but for now, get dressed so you're not late for school."

As soon as I said that, Sam jumped into my lap. "I'm sorry, Mommy. I don't hate you. I don't know why I said that. I really do love you."

Holding back tears, brought on not only by my frustration with Sam's behavior but also by the love I felt at that moment for my out-of-control daughter, I said, "Oh, Sammy, I love you too. Now go get dressed."

Sam quickly pulled her crumpled clothes from the laundry basket and threw them on. The triumphant smile on her face made me hopeful that the rest of the morning would go much smoother. That hope quickly vanished, and the knot in my stomach returned as we walked down the steps toward the kitchen. I realized we were out of her favorite Pop-Tart flavor. Unfortunately, Sam's outbursts were not limited to clothes.

Seconds later, a new tirade began, leaving me emotionally drained before the day even started. In an attempt to avoid situations like this in the future, I stocked up on Pop-Tarts and bought duplicates of Sam's favorite outfits. But no matter how hard I tried, there was always something new just waiting to set her off. Sam had entered the "terrible twos" with a bang, and now, much to my dismay, they were lasting much longer than expected.

After reading about this stage in various early childhood

development books, I learned that this phase could be extremely challenging for many parents. This was news to me since Dana had rarely exhibited the typical negative behaviors of the terrible twos. Needless to say, we were unprepared when Sam didn't miss a beat.

Unfortunately for our family, she checked off every indicator listed: *Display negative, defiant, and rebellious behavior as they struggle with their emerging independence; Without knowing how to verbalize their needs, throw temper tantrums and hit people; Object to things they used to be okay with; Mood swings where one minute they are happy and the next screaming and crying.*

Much to most parents' relief, this normal phase in a child's life is generally short-lived and usually outgrown by the time they reach the age of three. But we weren't so lucky. Sam didn't outgrow the "terrible twos" by age three or even age ten. Hers lasted until much, much later in life.

"Aimee, wait!"

I turned and saw the mom of one of Sam's preschool classmates approaching. With a smile on her face, she said, "I wanted to tell you that we give you a lot of credit for letting Sam come to school looking the way she does."

Speechless, I stared back at her in disbelief. Over time, I'd learned that allowing Sam to express herself by wearing the clothes and hairdo that made her feel comfortable, rather than insisting that she change her outfit or wear her hair in what I thought was a more attractive style, had two benefits: it prevented an argument, yes, but it also helped nurture her independence and self-confidence.

I had just dropped Sam at preschool in one of her favorite outfits—one that didn't exactly match but was, thankfully, clean—with her hair in a ponytail on top of her head like Paula Abdul wore in the eighties. I thought she looked adorable, but more importantly, she was happy.

After regaining my composure, and without a smile on my face, I pressed this rude mother, "So, who exactly are 'we'?"

"Oh," she said, her smile faltering a little bit, "some of the other moms and I noticed that you let Sam come to school in the same outfit days in a row. And her hair, well, you know."

Glaring back at her, I said, "Really, is that so? Well, maybe you and the other moms should consider that there are more important things in life for me to worry about than the clothes my child wears or the way she combs her hair." Without saying goodbye, I turned and walked away.

That wasn't the first time I'd had to defend my daughter's unconventional ways, and it definitely wouldn't be the last. After this altercation, I tried even harder to keep my arguments with Sam to more important issues, which, as she got older and became more confrontational on a much larger scale, grew in number.

"Mom, wait!"

I stopped and turned. Sam was standing in front of a store with her face pressed to the window. The girls and I had just seen a Raffi children's concert in New York City, and until that moment, we'd been singing and dancing our way back to our car, reliving our favorite songs from the show. If you're wondering if singing and dancing in public was the most embarrassing part of this story—regrettably, it wasn't.

Face still pressed against the window, Sam called out, "This place sells candy. Can we go in and get some? Please!?"

It had been a long day, and the girls had eaten a lot of food at the concert. "No," I said firmly. "You had enough to eat this afternoon, and I want to get on the road so we can avoid the traffic getting home."

Sam immediately dropped to the street and started yelling, "I hate you! I'm still hungry, so why can't I have candy now? That's not fair!"

This wasn't unusual since Sam's defiant behavior was not restricted to our home. Shopping, family outings, holiday meals, and play dates typically ended with her screaming and in tears and me frustrated, embarrassed, sometimes in tears also, and always wondering why. But this meltdown was on a whole new level.

Relentless and caught up in her tantrum, Sam wouldn't budge, so I ended up half-carrying and half-dragging my screaming, kicking child toward the car. While Dana stood back and watched in disgust as her sister ruined yet another special outing for all of us, I held back my tears and pushed forward.

And then I saw the familiar faces of a friend and his daughter heading right toward us.

I was so humiliated that I wanted to hide behind a parked car. Since that was impossible, I just acted like I hadn't seen them and kept walking, a wailing Sam still fighting me every step of the way.

I'm not quite sure how I heard his voice above Sam's continued crying and whining about the candy when he called out, "Aimee, hi! Were you and the girls at the Raffi concert?"

I turned around, and over Sam's commotion, said, "Yes, wasn't it great?"

He must have read the embarrassment written all over my face because after I replied, he said, "It sure was. Listen, I'm sorry we can't stay to talk more, but we're in a hurry to get home. See you soon!"

They waved good-bye and continued on their way, leaving me feeling helpless and a bit mortified. It was humiliating enough for strangers to have witnessed Sam's outburst, but playing out the scene in front of people I knew made it that much worse.

For years to come, I reflected on that day—without a doubt, one of my most embarrassing parenting moments—with a heavy heart. What could I have done differently to have avoided the public drama created by Sam, Dana's disappointment, and my feelings of incompetence? I was never able to come up with a good answer to that question—but to this day, I use this incident as a barometer for how far we have come since.

I had hoped that Sam's troublesome behavior would disappear when she approached the age of three. But when her third birthday came and went, and things had gotten worse instead of better, I had the dreadful feeling that the "terrible twos" were here to stay.

I had a friend with a daughter two years older than Sam, who I knew had displayed similar traits when she was a toddler. While at a party one day in his backyard, I confided in him about Sam's unruly behavior.

"I hope you don't mind me asking," I said, "but I know you had trouble early on with your daughter, and I'm wondering how you coped with the 'terrible twos.'"

He smiled. "Of course, I don't mind. I think our girls are a lot alike—and believe me, it wasn't easy."

Hoping for a more encouraging response, I pressed, "Well, when did the 'terrible twos' end for your daughter?"

He looked at me with sympathetic eyes. "They didn't."

I'd begun the conversation hoping that he would alleviate my fears. Instead, he merely heightened my concerns.

5

DESPERATELY SEARCHING FOR ANSWERS

I HAVE FOUND THAT ONE OF the most difficult challenges of parenting a child with behavior problems is learning to ignore hurtful accusations and unsolicited, well-intentioned advice from friends, family members, and therapists. Before Sam was diagnosed with ADHD, I sensed that she had very little control over her actions, especially when she would spiral into an uncontrollable outburst over insignificant issues. Throughout her childhood, I often found myself defending my parenting decisions to those who thought I wasn't consistent or strict enough. Many times, that person was my husband, Barry, who often left me feeling alone in my desperate search for normalcy in our family.

I fell in love with Barry's kind heart and easygoing personality when we met in college. I admired his strong commitment to his family, his ability to take other people's feelings into consideration, and his effort to always do the right thing. I sensed from the beginning that Barry would be a hands-on father, and I hoped that he would be successful in instilling some of his values and outlook on life in our children when the time came for us to have a family.

When Dana was young, it became apparent that she had many of Barry's personality traits. Her even-tempered disposition and inherent ability to distinguish between right and wrong made it easy for

Barry to relate to our firstborn and helped lay the foundation for the strong bond they developed.

When Sam arrived twenty-six months later, I had an uncanny feeling that things might be very different between Barry and our younger daughter. Unfortunately, the dynamics I instinctively anticipated began to materialize as I witnessed his reaction to Sam's defiant personality. As Sam's tantrums escalated, I worried that her inability to control her emotions and behavior might jeopardize their ability to bond with one another.

Barry grew up in a household where he rarely talked back to his father or questioned his parents' motives when denied something he wanted. Naturally, he expected the same respect from his children. When that didn't happen with Sam, he became extremely frustrated. It didn't take long for Barry to realize that it wasn't easy being the father of a confrontational, argumentative, and often disrespectful child. But he didn't seem to know how to adjust to this reality.

One night, Barry and I were sitting on the living room couch watching TV while Sam was playing with her dolls on the floor and Dana was upstairs in her room, reading. An unusually calm evening in our household. When it got close to Sam's bedtime, however, the atmosphere abruptly changed.

Barry took the lead in getting her ready. "Hey, Sam," he said calmly, "it's time for bed. Time to put your toys away and start cleaning up."

She ignored his first request, so he tried again, but not as calmly as he had the first time. "Sam," he snapped. "Stop ignoring me and start putting away your toys. It's bedtime."

I was engrossed in the show we were watching and only half listening to their conversation, so I didn't realize what was brewing until I heard Sam yelling, "No! I don't have to listen to you. I don't want to go to bed now. I want to keep playing!"

Before I had a chance to intervene and try to calm things down,

Barry lost his temper and yelled back at her, "Sam, I'm not going to ask you again. You know it's your bedtime, so let's go NOW!"

Upset that she didn't get her way, Sam started crying and escaped to her room. She screamed, "I hate you!" before slamming the door behind her.

When Barry stood up and ran after Sam, I knew he wanted to punish her—that was the only way he knew how to regain his authority. Concerned with the way things had spiraled out of control and unsure of what would happen next if he reached Sam's room, I jumped up, stopped him halfway up the stairs, and challenged him to reconsider.

"Barry, please stop! Do you think that arguing with Sam or punishing her has worked in the past?"

He stopped and considered. "No, I guess not."

We sat down and talked.

"Why don't you shift gears and try a different approach?" I suggested. "I'm not quite sure what that approach should be right now, but I do know you need to stop inflaming the situation with Sam and try to find a more effective way of dealing with her outbursts."

It was obvious that Sam's lack of self-control and her innate capacity to create havoc in our house was a thorn in her father's side. As she challenged Barry every step of the way and managed to turn family gatherings into chaos, the friction between the two of them escalated. He worked long hours and resented the disruption that Sam often created when he got home at night and on weekends, the valued times when most working parents cherish spending quality time with their children. Although he tried to control his anger when Sam acted out, he was often visibly upset by her behavior and her in-his-face outbursts.

I was surprised by Barry's defeated attitude and the anger Sam elicited in him, which was extremely uncharacteristic. Where was the easygoing guy I'd met at college all those years ago? At times, he would throw up his hands in disgust and give in to her demands, declaring, "Okay, enough, you win." Other times he would scream at her when she ignored his simple requests and disrespected his authority. Unfortunately, neither approach worked. Rather than calming things down or causing Sam to change her behavior, it only exacerbated the situation and created more tension between the two of them.

Although I was able to de-escalate the situation between Barry and Sam that night, it would take many years for the two of them to fix their stormy relationship.

One day I had a work presentation to prepare for, so I asked my mother to come over and help me with the girls. She arrived with a smile on her face and love in her heart.

"Hello, my sweet Dana and Sam!" she greeted them cheerily. "I hear Mommy has work to do, so why don't we go upstairs and find something fun to play with?"

Off they went, with my mother following close behind. Pleased with how things were going, and hoping for a few hours of peace and quiet, I shut the door to my office and started working.

For a while, I heard the girls and my mother talking and laughing. Shortly after, they were in the kitchen looking for snacks. That's when things started to escalate.

"No, Grandma Glady, I want to bake cookies—I don't want the store-bought ones," Sam insisted, her voice growing louder with every word.

"Stop yelling at Grandma. She's just trying to help," Dana jumped in. "You're such a baby."

I was tempted to intervene, but I decided to see what my mother would do first. Her ability to approach situations with a loving heart and to parent without judgment were traits I had relied upon throughout my life. I had always hoped that I would be able to have the same positive influence on my children's lives that she'd had on mine.

Sam's behavior problems often made me doubt my parenting abilities, so I looked to my mother for advice. Although she lacked the hands-on experience of raising a child with behavior problems like Sam's, the support she provided during the difficult times was invaluable. Her nonjudgmental way allowed me to vent my frustrations and insecurities without feeling belittled or criticized.

I admired her ability to assume her role as a grandmother in a similar manner that she had motherhood. I was also impressed by how she always kept her composure while searching for ways to help Sam, especially since I sensed how much it pained her to witness our younger daughter's temper tantrums and disruptive behavior.

In this moment, as always, she kept her cool. "Well, Sam, unfortunately, we don't have all the ingredients to bake cookies," my mother explained calmly.

"So, let's go to the store and buy what we need. I told you I want to bake cookies!" Sam yelled back.

Instead of reprimanding Sam for yelling, my mother quietly offered an alternative. "I have an idea. Why don't we take the cookies from the bag in the pantry and put them in the oven to warm up? Then, we can put icing on them and top them with chocolate chips. I see we have both of those ingredients in the pantry. They will taste just like homemade ones! What do you say?"

As Sam pondered what her grandma had just proposed, there was a minute of silence. Then, in a happy tone this time, she answered, "Yessss! I love that idea, Gramma. I'm sorry I yelled at you!"

For the next hour, I heard the three of them talking and laughing again.

When I was finished with my work, I went to see what they were doing. The kitchen was clean, and the cookies all eaten, but no one was there. I decided to check upstairs in Sam's room, assuming they were playing with some of her toys. When I opened the door, I didn't see or hear anyone. I couldn't imagine where they were, so I stepped inside and turned—and found my mother and both girls sitting in Sam's crib with the side down.

"Surprise!" they yelled and then collapsed into giggles.

I will always think back to that day and the picture I took of the three of them sitting in Sam's crib as a reminder of how my mother was able to help her granddaughter out of a stressful situation and see things in a different light. Through it all, she showered Sam with love and affection and never passed judgment or made her feel inferior to her well-behaved older sister. Although I found it hard to maintain the same composure at times, I always tried to emulate her compassionate way of dealing with Sam. I believe the reason I was often successful was because I inherited that trait directly from my mother.

I had always loved going out for dinner with other couples on Saturday nights to unwind and spend quality time with Barry and our friends. As Sam's behavior problems emerged, however, the conversations at these dinners often became argumentative and directed toward me.

One night, over cocktails and appetizers at a restaurant with our close friends Michelle and Bruce, it happened despite my best efforts to keep our table talk on other topics.

"So," Michelle asked, during a brief lull in the conversation, "How's Sam doing in school these days?"

Trying not to offer too much, I replied, "She's okay. I have an appointment with her teacher this week."

Michelle took a sip of her drink. "What's the appointment about?"

"It seems like Sam missed a few homework assignments and has been interrupting her teacher," I explained reluctantly. "I'll find out more when we meet."

"Why do you think Sam is doing this?" she pressed on. "Don't you check her homework and reprimand her for interrupting people when they are talking?"

This had become a pattern in recent years—friends questioning my parenting methods and criticizing me for not being consistent or strict enough when disciplining Sam. Many times, I found myself retreating to the bathroom to hide my tears when these verbal barrages about my perceived parenting flaws became overwhelming.

Finding the strength to stick up for myself, I said, "Actually, I'm beginning to wonder if Sam has a disability like ADHD or if it has something to do with her being jealous of Dana."

Relentlessly, Michelle continued, "Maybe the problem with Sam is not related to a disability or sibling rivalry. Instead of looking for an excuse for her behavior, maybe you should consider that the problem could be that Sam acts the way she does because you are an ineffective disciplinarian." She stared at me from across the table. "I'm sure that Sam would respond better if she was afraid of you and feared the repercussions of her actions."

Feeling completely defenseless, I looked to Barry for help. But he just sat there, saying nothing. His silence and lack of support spoke volumes.

I was having a hard time holding back tears, but before escaping to the bathroom, I mustered up the courage to offer my own hypothesis: "Did you ever think that Sam might be acting out and lying to us about her schoolwork because she finds it difficult to concentrate and has trouble controlling her emotions? And following in her sister's footsteps is probably contributing to her insecurities as well?" Feeling completely overwhelmed, I stood up. "And maybe it really *is* ADHD or some other disability?" I added before excusing myself from the table and escaping to the closest lady's room, where I broke down in tears.

I knew there was more to the story than what everyone else was seeing and accusing me of, but the reason wasn't clear to me yet. And as I sat on the closed toilet, composing myself, I decided that I would keep doing what *I* thought was right for *my* child. Although I honestly believe my friend did not mean to upset me, her words hurt, and her criticism made me doubt myself. Still, I was determined to never waver in my beliefs—regardless of what others thought of me.

"Dana, I'm bored," Sam whined. "Don't you want to play a game with me?"

We were driving to my mother-in-law's cousin's apartment in New York City for Thanksgiving—one of the busiest traffic days of the year. Our choice had been to stay home, just the four of us, or join our family at Ruth's and take the chance that the roads wouldn't be as bad as predicted. We'd decided on the latter, but now we were five miles away from the Lincoln Tunnel with traffic at a standstill.

Up until that point, Sam and Dana had been entertaining themselves in the backseat, listening to music and playing games. But the hour delay getting to the tunnel was pushing Sam over the edge. She'd had enough.

Dana shook her head. "No, Sam. Can't you see I'm reading?" she said without even looking up from her book.

Without skipping a beat, Sam started to cry. "You're the worst sister," she yelled. "I hate you, Dana!" Then she looked at me. "Mom, I'm hungry. Can I have another granola bar?"

When I realized we had run out of granola bars, I had Barry find a place to pull over so I could switch seats with Dana and try to draw Sam out of her funk. Stuck in our car with such limited supplies, I had little to work with. Luckily for all of us, Sam cried herself to sleep before we got through the tunnel, giving us a reprieve for what was left of our ride. Hoping this nap would put her in a better mood when we arrived, I, too, closed my eyes and tried to center myself. Thanksgiving has always been my favorite holiday, and I didn't want Sam to ruin it for me or my family with a meltdown.

∿

Sam woke up as we pulled into the parking garage, and the look on her face told me that not much had changed. Hoping that her mood would improve after she ate something, I put her coat on and guided my unhappy child to the elevator.

Upon entering the apartment, Dana ran off to see her grandparents. When I noticed how hot it was inside and realized that Sam was overdressed, my heart sank into my stomach—my younger child was extremely sensitive to temperature changes. It didn't take long for Sam to start complaining about the heat.

"Mom, it's too hot in here," she whimpered. "Can we go home now?"

"You know we can't," I said quietly. "It's Thanksgiving, and we just got here."

At that, Sam started to cry and then, in front of everyone, began to take off her clothes in the middle of the living room. Determined to avoid a scene, I marched Sam into the bathroom and removed her tights and turtleneck, hoping that would do the trick. Trying to keep my composure in check, I put a smile on my face and led Sam back to join our family. I could tell that Barry was annoyed at Sam for her outbursts in the car, but I couldn't deal with this all evening on my own—I needed his help.

"She's out of control," I whispered to him. "Can we take turns entertaining her until dinner is served? Please!"

He rolled his eyes and walked off with Sam without a word. I stood there for a minute, trying to process what had just happened: Sam out of control and Barry acting as if it was my fault. *What the hell?* Anger was building up, but I was not wanting to have an argument in front of others, so I just walked over to the bar and reached for a glass of wine. The discussion with Barry would have to wait until we got home later that night.

~

Unfortunately, dinner wasn't much better. Sam didn't like what was being served, refused to sit at the table, and kept insisting that she wanted to watch a video we didn't have with us. A tantrum followed each disappointment.

Trying not to ruin everyone else's Thanksgiving more than we already had, Barry, Dana, and I quickly ate our meal and then excused ourselves. Heading to the elevator—Sam crying, Dana upset we had to leave so early, and Barry being Barry—I held back my anger as a myriad of emotions poured through my body.

Even though no one had made a direct criticism of my parenting that evening, I always felt judged when Sam cried and threw temper tantrums like that in front of others. I sensed that everyone, including Barry, expected me to calm her down and defuse the disruptive outbursts. After all, isn't that what a good mother does when her child is acting out? But I couldn't always do that, so my solution was to simply remove my out-of-control child from the situation, assuming all the while that everyone left behind was talking about us and, undoubtedly, thinking I was the source of Sam's problems. Driving home with Sam sulking in the backseat, I couldn't help but wonder if it really was my fault. How could I not?

When we got home and the girls were in bed, I started an overdue conversation with Barry. "So, let me explain how I felt tonight when I asked you to help with Sam when she was acting out at dinner," I began. "Not sure if you realize it, but you rolled your eyes at me and walked off with Sam with an annoyed look on your face. Just so you know, those nonverbal reactions to situations like this make me feel alone in our struggles with Sam. It's a similar feeling I get when you are silent when our friends are blaming me for her problems and you sit there without defending me or saying anything."

"I don't remember rolling my eyes," Barry said without emotion. "I think you are overreacting. It is true I was upset with Sam, but I didn't think I was acting annoyed toward you. I'm sorry if that's what you thought."

Clearly, we were not on the same page when it came to Sam. This was something we had to work on.

Years later, I found out that Barry's cousin had vivid memories of that Thanksgiving. Although we had tried to defuse the situation by leaving early, she admitted that the people left behind were, in fact, talking about us. She said it was painful for everyone to watch Sam's inability to cope and our failed attempts to help her. Although she didn't specifically blame me for Sam's problems, I was taken aback when she noted how uncomfortable it was for her to watch the tension between Barry and me. It upset me to know that we weren't able to hide it as well as I would have liked. The reason we were having that conversation in the first place, however, was because she had observed a drastic improvement in Sam's behavior and the way Barry and I handled similar situations at subsequent holiday meals and family gatherings—and that fact gave me tremendous solace.

When it came to family members, my mother-in-law, Carol, was my biggest challenge. Throughout Sam's early childhood, I was often confused by her disapproving attitude toward her younger granddaughter. I would have expected her training and experiences as a special education teacher to be an asset when it came to dealing with Sam, but that wasn't the case. Although she did not outwardly verbalize her disapproval of Sam's negative behavior or my inability to control my daughter, her facial expressions, body language, and tone of voice spoke volumes.

As difficult as it was dealing with Sam's unruly disposition during family meals, holiday celebrations, and vacations, what made things extremely uncomfortable for me was constantly feeling judged by Carol during events that included her. Although it may not have been her intention, every time Sam interrupted a conversation, cried when things didn't go her way, or failed to do what someone asked, Carol radiated a negativity in my direction that made me question everything I said or did in front of her. She acted perpetually annoyed at the commotion Sam created and seemed to resent the fact that her granddaughter singlehandedly put a damper on many of our family gatherings.

When Carol offered to take the four of us to Disneyland when Sam was five and Dana seven, I was hesitant because of the friction that existed between Sam and her grandma and the gnawing resentment I had been feeling toward her in recent months. I also questioned whether Disney was the right environment for a child who typically had unpredictable meltdowns in new situations. But I'd heard from multiple people that Disney vacations always resulted in cherished family memories, so against my better judgment, I said yes.

As soon we arrived at the hotel, I began to realize that accepting Carol's invitation had almost certainly been a big mistake. After checking in at the front desk, we approached the glass elevator that would take us to our tenth-floor rooms. Unexpectedly, Sam pulled back from the elevator and started to cry.

"Stop!" she moaned. "I'm scared of getting into this elevator. You can see outside the whole way up instead of it being inside the building! Can't we get a room on the first floor instead? PLEASE?"

Since Carol preferred the nicer view that came with a room on a higher floor, she tried first. "Oh, Sam, it's not scary," she insisted. "You'll only be in it for a little while."

"Nope, I won't get in!" Sam blurted out as tears rolled down her cheeks. "You can keep your room on the higher floor, but I won't go."

Hoping to calm Sam down and put her in a better mood going forward—but much to Carol's disappointment—we changed rooms to the first floor and crossed our fingers.

After settling into our new rooms, we headed out to the Magic Kingdom Park. We bought tickets and then walked toward Under the Sea ~ Journey of The Little Mermaid. As we approached, I saw the look on Sam's face and knew we were in trouble.

As soon as she saw a picture of Ursula, the Sea Witch, she hid behind me and started to cry. "O-M-G, I hate Ursula! She's so mean and scary. I can't go on this ride! I want to go back to the hotel."

Realizing I wasn't going to be able to convince Sam to change her mind, I suggested I take her to a different section of the park with smaller, less "scary" rides while Barry took Dana to the ones that she would enjoy.

What to do with Carol was my next problem to solve. Since she wouldn't go on the rides with Dana and Barry, she elected to join Sam and me, even though she was visibly losing her patience with her younger granddaughter. We made it through a few of the rides with Sam and then worked our way back to the hotel. By the time we arrived at our room, Sam was completely exhausted and not a happy camper.

I tried to lighten the mood and start to get her ready for dinner before Dana and Barry got back. "Hey Sammy, let's get you undressed and into the shower—we have a fun dinner planned," I said with my fingers crossed behind my back.

"I don't want to shower, and I don't want to go to dinner," she grumbled. "I'm too tired. I wish we could go home. I don't like it here."

At that moment, I remembered reading about a babysitting room at the hotel called the Lollipop Lounge. Trying to remain optimistic, I picked up the phone and set up a time for us to bring Sam there while we had dinner. Luckily, after showing her pictures of where we wanted her to go, she went agreeably—and when we picked her up after our meal, she ran into my arms and, with a big smile on her face, said, "This was great! I love it here."

What a relief. We'd managed to overcome one major challenge.

But as our Disney vacation went on and Sam repeatedly refused to shower, go on rides, or eat dinner with us, I felt anger building—not in me but in Carol. It was written all over my mother-in law's face and evident in the way she reacted to Sam. Of course, I understood why Carol was upset since we all felt the consequences of Sam's disruptive behavior. But I wished she could have been more supportive and less judgmental. It would have been nice to have her to confide in back then and throughout the trying times of Sam's childhood. I guess I should have trusted my gut instincts. In the end, our Disney vacation failed to produce cherished family memories. If anything, it did just the opposite!

Had Carol's attitude toward her younger granddaughter been limited to my own discomfort and not outwardly affected Sam, I would have overlooked many of her indiscretions, but the protective mother in me sensed differently. It didn't take long for Sam's intuitive nature to kick in and feel that her Grandma Carol did not treat her with the same love and affection she displayed toward her well-behaved older sister. There were times I suspected that Sam purposefully acted out in front of her grandmother because she didn't know how to verbalize her true feelings.

One day when Sam was five years old, and we were lying on her bed together, she asked me, "Why does Grandma Carol treat me so differently than Dana? I think she loves Dana more than me."

I felt that it wasn't up to me to convince Sam otherwise, and Carol happened to be sitting in our living room at the time. So, I walked downstairs to tell her what was going on.

"Carol, would you mind coming upstairs to talk to Sam?" I asked. "She's upset about some things relating to you, so I was hoping you could help her see things differently."

We walked into Sam's room together, and I started the conversation by asking, "Sam, can you tell Grandma what you told me a little while ago?"

Sam looked down at the floor and sheepishly said, "I want to know why you treat Dana differently than you do me. It seems like you don't love me as much as Dana."

Instead of finding a way to ease her granddaughter's insecurities, Carol merely said, "Oh, Sam, of course, I love you as much as Dana." She then shot me an angry look and quickly left the room.

When I followed her downstairs, Carol proceeded to turn the blame on me. "I can't believe you did this to me," she snapped. "It's pretty clear that Sam is trying to manipulate you into feeling sorry for her. You shouldn't have included me in such an embarrassing conversation."

At the time, I was extremely disappointed in the outcome and felt that Carol wasn't willing to take any of the responsibility for the poor state of her relationship with Sam. But in hindsight, I realize that putting her on the spot the way I did was probably wrong. I wonder how things might have turned out had I tried to talk to my mother-in-law beforehand instead of bringing her upstairs and challenging her in front of Sam.

Regrettably, I will never know the answer to that question, and for the next sixteen years, I painfully watched the relationship between Sam and her grandma get much worse before it got better.

6

DOCTORS AND THERAPISTS AND TEACHERS, OH MY!

During Sam's early childhood, I discovered that conventional discipline didn't work. Punishments were ineffective, and time-outs meant nothing to my defiant daughter. Threatening to take something away from Sam or not allowing her to go places she was looking forward to never made a lasting impression, either.

After our failed Disney vacation, it was clear that Barry and I needed a new approach with our younger daughter. Due to Barry's demanding work schedule, I took on the responsibility of finding that approach.

My first attempt began with a visit to our pediatrician. He suggested that I talk to a family psychologist in hopes of finding a solution before things got out of control.

Hmmm, I'm pretty sure they're already out of control! I thought to myself.

He gave me the name and phone number of someone he thought we should try. I left his office feeling somewhat optimistic. At least I had a plan for a new approach. When I got home, I took a deep breath and dialed the number.

"Hello, this is Aimee Kaufman. My daughter is having behavior problems that are difficult for my husband and me to handle. Our pediatrician suggested that I call you to set up an appointment."

"Hello, Mrs. Kaufman. Thanks for calling," the psychologist said. "I'm sorry to hear about your problems with your daughter. I have an opening next week, but please come alone. We can decide if you need to bring your daughter after our first meeting."

I have to admit I was confused about why I was being told to leave Sam at home since her behavioral issues were what I hoped to address, but I assumed there was a good reason, so I made the appointment.

The next week, sitting on a couch in the psychologist's office, I began the conversation with our family history.

"So, to give you a little background about my family, Sam is our younger child. She has a sister named Dana, who is two years older. My husband, Barry, and I began noticing that Sam started acting out when she was about two years old, and it's been getting worse as the years go by." I sighed. "She's five now and throws temper tantrums over minor things, like what clothes she wants to wear, what we are having for dinner, getting ready for bed, and almost anything, anytime and anywhere. She and Dana have been fighting a lot over what TV show to watch, who goes first at anything, and where to sit in the car, to name just a few issues. I'm concerned that she might have ADHD or some other behavioral disability since we haven't been able to figure out what triggers her outbursts."

After spending an hour describing the difficulties we were having and how Sam managed to disrupt our lives on a daily basis, the psychologist, who had been listening intently, explained what she thought the problem was.

"Well, it seems to me that the problem in the Kaufman household is sibling rivalry," she said. "Sam is most likely acting out because of her jealousy of her older sister. I suggest that you read *Siblings Without Rivalry*. This should help you to help Sam."

I was surprised that she was able to make this diagnosis without meeting Sam and Dana. I also had doubts that this was the underlying problem in our family. But she was the professional, so I drove straight to the bookstore, hoping for the best.

I have to admit, I did learn some valuable lessons from *Siblings Without Rivalry*, and after reading it cover to cover, I was eager to implement some of the suggested strategies, hoping that doing so would bring some much-needed peace and quiet to our home.

Unfortunately, it didn't take long to realize that it wasn't going to be that easy. I tried to acknowledge Sam's feelings and not take sides or compare her to Dana, but the behavior problems persisted and seemed to be getting worse. Dana's and Sam's dilemma.

Strike one!

I decided to change directions and seek advice from the director of Sam's preschool since he was aware of some of her behavior issues in the classroom. When I told him about her defiant behavior at home and how she didn't respond to punishment, he suggested that we turn the doorknob around and lock her in her bedroom when that happens. He had a degree in childhood *something*, so, although I was unsure about his suggestion, I trusted his judgment. *Worth a try, anyway*, I thought. I went home, grabbed a screwdriver, and turned the handle around so the lock to Sam's bedroom was on the outside.

The very next day, when Sam refused to put her toys away before dinner and started to yell at me, I jumped into action.

"Hey, that's enough, Sam. Stop yelling and go up to your room until you're ready to listen," I said in what I hoped was a calm voice.

"You're so mean," Sam yelled back at me. But to my surprise, she went to her room and slammed the door behind her. I then ran up and hesitantly turned the lock.

Sam must have heard the click of the lock because she immediately ran over and tried to open the door. When she discovered she couldn't, instead of lying down on her bed or doing something to calm herself, she began to sob uncontrollably.

"Let me out!" she screamed. "I can't believe you locked me in my room like this. I hate you so much!" As the sobbing got louder, she started to hyperventilate. In between her gasping for air, she cried, "I ... can't ... breathe!"

Feeling like a horrible mother, I immediately opened the door and took Sam into my arms. My heart ached for my out-of-control daughter more than ever.

When she calmed down, I let go. "I'm sorry I locked you in your room without explaining to you why and when I would do that," I told her. "But we definitely need to find a way to help you stay in control when you are upset or angry about things. I hope you know how much I love you."

Sam hugged me and, in a sheepish voice, said, "I'm sorry, Mommy. I don't hate you. I don't know why I say things like that to you. I love you so much."

I hugged her again, holding back my own tears.

Obviously, this approach made things worse, not better. I was just so desperate to help Sam gain control of her emotions and actions that I was willing to try anything. Having seen how she reacted, though, I definitely would not use the locked-door method on her ever again.

Strike two!

Trying not to feel defeated, I continued on my quest. I found another therapist, and this one at least wanted to include Sam in the first session this time. My initial feeling was optimistic. Sam and I both found Dr. Fischer to be very formal in his suit and tie, and his office was uncomfortable. We stuck with it for a few months, but eventually, I realized that Sam wasn't getting anything out of her sessions with him, and neither was I. He'd told me that he would be presenting his analysis of Sam at our next meeting. I decided that I would hear him out, but after that, it would be time to move on.

During this final session, Dr. Fischer determined that Sam did *not* have ADHD. Actually, I'm not exactly sure what his diagnosis was because virtually everything he said went way over my head. But he did make one final suggestion that heightened my interest: "I highly recommend that you implement positive reinforcement charts for Sam," he said. "Many parents of children with similar challenges find them to be useful."

I drove home feeling disappointed once again, but I decided to try the charts he had suggested. After all, what did I have to lose?

At home, I brought a whiteboard and some markers we had in our basement up to Sam's room and hung the board on her door, thinking that would be the easiest way for her to follow her own progress. The first chart said if she could go seven days without yelling at me, I would take her to Toys"R"Us and buy her a new toy. I drew seven boxes for Sam or me to check off upon the completion of a successful day. Another said if she could go seven days without fighting with Dana, she could stay up half an hour later on the weekends. When I was done, I went to find Sam.

"Hey, Sammy, can you come up to your room for a few minutes?" I asked her. "I want to show you something I think you will like."

Sam came running upstairs after me, but she stopped when she saw the board hanging on her door. "What's this?" she asked hesitantly.

"The therapist suggested we try a 'positive reinforcement chart' to help you gain control of your emotions and outbursts," I explained. "You've told me you don't know why you yell at me or fight with Dana, so I thought this might be a good way for you to try and work on this."

She looked skeptical, but I forged ahead and read the two things she had to do—actually, to *not* do—to earn a reward.

When she heard the word "reward," a big smile replaced her hesitant look. "Okay, Mommy. I'll try really hard! I already know what toy I want, and that would be great if I could stay up a little later on the weekends!"

Optimism exploded in my chest. *Maybe this will actually work!*

After the first week, I was excited to see some improvement. There were four boxes filled in for not yelling at me and three boxes for not fighting with Dana. Although not perfect, Sam was definitely showing progress.

It took another week for the other three boxes to be checked off for not yelling at me, but as soon as they were, off to Toys"R"Us we went! It took a little longer to get to the seven days without fighting with Dana, but eventually, Sam made it, and she was excited to be able to stay up a half hour later on the weekends.

Unfortunately, the positive changes didn't last very long. After a few weeks, Sam went back to her old ways. One morning, when I ran out of her favorite cereal, she lashed out at me once again. "I can't believe you didn't get more cereal when you went to the store yesterday! You know how much I like Fruit Loops. You're such a bad mom."

Trying to control myself and not show my disappointment, I replied, "Let's find something else so you're not late for school. You know how upset you get when the other kids are all there before you."

As for arguing and fighting with Dana—it didn't take long for Sam to revert back to her old ways there, either. It appeared that she lost interest in the rewards after those first few weeks.

As the negative behaviors crept back into our daily lives, we found ourselves back at square one.

Strike three!

But I have always found life to be more forgiving than the rigid rules of baseball, so I refused to walk away defeated—despite the fact that this most recent failure felt to me like strike three in the bottom of the ninth.

When Sam moved on to elementary school, I pushed the locked-bedroom-door episode to the back of my mind and decided to seek advice from her teachers and administrators. I often asked if they thought she had ADHD. It was a disability I knew very little about at the time, but based on what I did know, it seemed like it could explain the problems we were having with Sam at home. At school, though, Sam managed to keep her grades in line and rarely displayed similar behaviors—so, inevitably, the answer was always no.

But I kept going back to one incident that made me believe there was definitely more to Sam's problem than had been diagnosed so far. It happened on a work day when I was leaving her with a sitter, and for a reason I don't recall, she didn't want me to go. "F— you, Mom!" she raged. "I hate you and hope you die, and if you leave the house, I'm going to kill myself!"

Startled by her outburst, I reprimanded her for using the F-word, but I knew in my heart that she didn't mean what she had said. No matter how bad things got, I always believed that Sam loved me "to the sky and back." I had read at some point early on that even if their issues relate to someone or something else, children often aim their anger and frustration at their mother because they know—or at least hope—that she is the one person who will always love them no matter what. It was important for me to remember this during Sam's innumerable tirades; it often helped me to try not to take her outbursts so personally. I surmised that many kids say similar things to their mothers when they are at a loss for what to do or how to express their needs.

Sam threatening to hurt herself, however—that terrified me. Her disturbing words struck a chord deep inside my core. I called in sick to work that day and immediately sought advice from a professional.

I was feeling desperate and alarmed that afternoon when I took Sam to see our pediatrician, Dr. Cohen, but she reassured me that she did not see signs of a child who would harm herself.

"I think Sam is just lashing out at you because she's hurting inside," she said. "But it's also clear that she trusts you to be there for her when things settle down."

Keeping this advice in mind, going forward, I forced myself to walk out the door each time something similar happened. But the first time I did that, I sat in my car in the garage for a long time, trying to calm myself and debating whether or not I had done the right thing by leaving. *What if the doctor was wrong?* This was something no parent would want to think about, so I pushed the devastating thought out of my mind as I reluctantly backed out of the driveway and drove away. It was, undoubtedly, one of the most painful parenting decisions I ever had to make.

To convince myself I was making the right decisions during these troubling times, I focused on the fact that after Sam calmed down, she would always tell me that she was sorry, that she didn't know why she acted the way she did, she didn't mean what she had said, and that she loved me. Knowing that she meant every word, I could feel her pain and sense her regret for acting so poorly. I knew she wanted to change, and I came to realize that I was one of the few people in her life who, in spite of everything, believed in her completely, no matter what.

Sam validated my belief in her confidence in me while we were driving in the car one day. After listening to a Cyndi Lauper song, "True Colors," on the radio, she turned and looked at me with loving eyes and said, "Mommy, you are the only one who sees my true colors shining through."

So, painful as it often was, the protective mother in me continually jumped into action as my unwavering, unconditional love fueled my journey to finding help for my daughter.

∿

I wasn't the only one in our family suffering from Sam's continued outbursts and undiagnosed problems. It hurt me to watch as her relationship with Dana was affected as well.

I hate my sister! She is mean. Today would have been the perfect day if she weren't alive. I am not saying I want her to die, I just wish she was never born in the first place . . . She gets in trouble all the time and is just plain MEAN . . . Sam hit me a couple of times and it really hurt. I wish I didn't have a sister! She is DUMB, MEAN, SELFISH, AN IDIOT, STUPID, AND WEIRD. If you look those words up in the dictionary you would find a picture of Samantha Lynn Kaufman.

Dana wrote these entries in her diary when she was nine and Sam was seven. She went on to write, *I don't know why she does it . . . Mom says sometimes when I do something Sam can't, but she tries anyway. She gets jealous and is mean to me. I don't get her sometimes, and I don't want to.*

When Dana found her diary packed away in our basement and shared these entries with me years later, I could tell her memories were painful. She was visibly upset and reluctant to take ownership of the words she'd written in reaction to her sister's negative behavior. I had to sit down when I read these words for the first time, even though we were in a much better place by the time she showed them to me. I'd known back then that Dana was often hurt and confused by Sam's disruptive conduct, but I'd never realized at the time how deep her resentment was.

It made sense that she struggled with her emotions. Dana adored her sister from the moment she was born. She took on her role as the older sibling with pride, and she always tried to offer Sam advice and attempted to become someone Sam might look up to as they got older. But Sam had a hard time showing her love for Dana and often made her sister the main target of her daily outbursts.

Unfortunately, as Sam became the center of (negative) attention in our household, Dana took a backseat. When her relationship with her sister did not develop as she would have liked, she wrestled with her feelings and turned to her diary for comfort.

As I read through her entries and we discussed what led her to write those angry, heartfelt words, I went from feeling raw and upset to feeling extremely proud of her. It took a lot of restraint for Dana, at such a young age, to find a way to channel her anger into her writing instead of seeking revenge by saying or doing something she might have regretted later on.

During the early years when Dana and Sam would argue, I tried not to intervene, but it was hard not to when it was happening numerous times a day. Sam pulling something she wanted out of Dana's hand, the two of them fighting over what TV show to watch, who was going to sit in the front seat of the car, whether we'd go to McDonald's or Burger King or have ice cream or cookies for dessert . . . it went on and on and on. Although these appear to be typical arguments between siblings, Barry and I were at our wits' end due to the frequency and intensity of their disagreements.

Continuing to search for a solution, I looked back at some of the parenting books I had purchased and found a suggestion that I had overlooked earlier. The recommendation was to assign odd or even days of the month to each of the girls and allow them to make decisions that typically ended in an argument. Since Sam was born on an even day and Dana an odd one, I sat the girls down and explained how this would work.

"Since Sam's birthday is on the fourth, she will have even days to decide on what TV show to watch, for example," I announced. "Since Dana's is on the twenty-first, she will have odd days to make decisions like that. On months that have 31 days, that will be my day to decide. This way, you will each have an equal number of days."

Much to my surprise, the girls loved this approach, and in the months that followed, they consistently asked, "Whose day is it?"—thus avoiding an argument that would have developed previously.

I was thrilled that this new rule reduced the fighting over making these types of decisions, but unfortunately, that didn't help Sam's ability to control her emotions when things didn't go her way in other situations. Getting angry with Barry and me and throwing temper tantrums when she didn't want to do something continued, while fights with Dana over other issues seemed to escalate.

By the time Sam reached fourth grade, still with no diagnosis in sight, her astute teacher called to tell me she thought there was more of a problem than others had perceived. She informed us that Sam wasn't paying attention in class and was having trouble completing assignments. In addition, she was sometimes argumentative with her friends and disrespectful to her teachers. With heightened concern and in desperate hopes of finding a conclusive diagnosis, we finally decided to have Sam tested for ADHD.

Sam lacked many of the typical overt hyperactivity symptoms—constantly being on the go and excessively running or climbing at inappropriate times. Though she did display less obvious indications, such as biting her nails, sucking on her shirtsleeve, and fidgeting with small items, that hadn't been enough to indicate ADHD to her teachers in the past. Now, however, with this new teacher encouraging us to test her, I was eager to see what a professional had to say.

We chose not to go through the school system because we were told it would take months to initiate and complete the testing process (this was 1995; perhaps that wouldn't be the case today). Instead, we found a private "specialist" who came highly recommended by a new therapist we began seeing that year.

The specialist, Mr. Richards, got right to the point when I called: "Let me explain how this is going to work, Mrs. Kaufman. I will meet with Sam for three two-hour sessions and then talk to you and your husband to get your input on the issues you are observing. I will accumulate my findings and analysis and prepare a report for you to review."

"That sounds great," I replied, happy to have a clear plan. "We will schedule appointments with your assistant and look forward to getting things started."

I wasn't able to stay in the room with Sam during her appointments, so I didn't know exactly what went on. After her third session, Barry and I met with the evaluator for an hour to discuss our issues with Sam's behavior. Mr. Richards informed us that it might take a week or so to get back to us with his analysis, so I waited with bated breath for a call to set up our next appointment.

I received that call from his receptionist a week after our appointment and set up a time to meet the next day. But what he had to say at that meeting was not at all what I expected.

"So, I took all of the information I gathered from my meetings with Sam and you both, then put them into my computer program," he told us. "It showed that Sam does not have ADHD after all. I do believe she has some learning disabilities, however, and that she might be depressed. I have everything printed out here for you to have and to show to her teachers if you like."

Hearing this, I deflated like a balloon. "Okay, thank you for your time and this information," I said, unable to hide my disappointment. "I will set up a meeting at her school to discuss your diagnosis."

When we walked out of his office, I almost lost it. I was so confused and let down by the outcome. I looked at my husband with tears in my eyes and blurted out, "I cannot believe this. This is the third person who's decided that Sam doesn't have ADHD. But, after reading about it, she shows so many of the symptoms. I'll call the school when we get home and set up an appointment with her teacher and the special ed supervisor. Maybe they can shed some light on the situation. Ugh!"

Unfortunately, when Sam's teacher and the special ed supervisor read the computer-generated report, they were as confused as I was. Together, we tried to figure out what the best course of action was for Sam, but we didn't get anywhere new.

With no answers or help in sight, Sam moved on to fifth grade.

Around the time when Sam and Dana were old enough to stay home alone—or so I thought—I was at work when my cell phone rang. I immediately answered when I saw it was Dana calling. Hearing her crying and Sam screaming at her in the background, I tamped down my anger, shut my office door, and tried to find out what happened.

In what I thought was a controlled voice, I asked Dana, "Are you okay? What's going on? Why is Sam yelling at you?"

Choking back her sobs, Dana replied, "Sam wants me to play with her, but I have lots of homework. She started yelling at me and insisting that I stop and come downstairs. She is so mean and I can't take it. You have to come home now!"

Still trying to stay calm, I said, "I'll be home in fifteen minutes. Tell Sam she better get herself under control before I get home."

Frustration at a boil, I let my boss know there was an emergency at home and rushed out to my car.

I was surprised by the silence that greeted me as I opened the front door when I arrived home.

Upon walking up the stairs into the living room, I discovered Sam wrapped in a blanket, camped out in her favorite sanctuary: the living room couch.

"Hi Sam, what's going on?" I asked.

When she didn't answer, I turned around and looked up to the bedroom level—and saw a hole in Dana's door. Glancing back at Sam, knowing in my heart that she was the instigator who had created that hole, I decided to check on Dana before figuring out what my next move would be.

I went upstairs but found Dana's door locked; she was hiding from her sister. I knocked. "Dana, it's Mom. Can you please open the door so I can come in and talk to you?"

Holding back tears, Dana replied, "Okay, as long as Sam isn't with you."

"She's downstairs on the couch," I assured her.

Dana unlocked the door, and we both sat on her bed.

"Mom, she's impossible!" she blurted out. "I was in my room doing my homework when Sam came up and wanted me to go downstairs to play a video game with her. I told her I would after I finished my homework, but she started yelling at me and tried to throw my books on the floor. Somehow, I got her to leave my room, so I locked her out. All of a sudden, I heard her kicking my door and yelling at me to let her in again. I didn't know what to do, so that's when I called you to come home."

Before I went down to talk to Sam, I tried to console Dana. "Oh, Danes, I'm so sorry this happened. Hopefully, we'll find a way to help Sam control her emotions soon so she doesn't lash out at you when things don't go her way. I love you! I'll go talk to Sam now."

As I walked out of Dana's room, I turned and looked at the hole in her door. Realizing this argument had ended in such a violent way raised my concern about Sam's behavior and added to my frustration. Taking deep breaths, I went downstairs, determined to try my best to have a peaceful conversation with my complicated younger daughter.

I sat down next to Sam on the couch and began. "Hi there, Sam. Dana told me what happened, so now I want you to tell me your side of the story. What got you so mad that you kicked a hole in her door?"

In a remorseful voice, Sam tried to explain. "Oh, Mom, I'm so sorry. I don't know why I got so mad. I was bored and wanted Dana to play a video game with me. When she said no and that she had to finish her homework, I started to yell at her. I didn't want to wait. Then I tried to throw her books on the floor and make her come downstairs with me. When she locked me out of her room, I got so angry that I started kicking the door. When I realized that I made a hole with my sneaker, I ran downstairs and hid under the blanket on the couch. When I heard her call you at work, I knew you would be really mad at me, so I tried to calm down and leave Dana alone. I'm really sorry. I just couldn't stop myself."

With a lump in my throat, I gathered her into my arms. "Oh, Sammy, of course, I'm disappointed about what happened and worried that you chose to lash out at Dana and her door the way you did. But the first thing you said to me, that you don't know why you got so mad, makes me wonder if we are missing something. The doctors, therapists, and school administrators haven't been able to figure out why you are acting this way, but I'm not going to give up trying to help you gain control of your emotions. I promise. I am more worried than mad at you." I gave her a big hug, then pulled back a little and looked her in the eyes. "Can you do me a favor and go apologize to Dana, please? And know that I love you."

Throughout this entire ordeal, from the call from Dana to me at my office to my conversations with the girls, I tried really hard to keep my cool and not let my anger take over. And I thought I had done a pretty good job of it—until I received a call from my boss checking to make sure I'd made it home safely. Apparently, while I thought I was speaking calmly to Dana, I had actually been yelling into the phone, and when I left, I had run out in such a hurry that he was worried I might get into an accident on my way home.

His concern was a wake-up call for me. It forced me to dig deep and try harder going forward to control my anger and to find alternative ways to help fix what I perceived as Dana and Sam's broken relationship. It also made me realize that as hard as it sometimes was being Sam's mom, being her sister wasn't easy either.

Regrettably, this was not an isolated incident. Confrontations like this created an ongoing problem for Dana on a daily basis. Sam's big, boisterous personality dominated our attention, and her combative nature often caused her sister to escape to her room for refuge. During these times, I felt sad for both of my girls: Dana for having to tolerate Sam's disruptive behavior and Sam for not having the ability to control her actions that typically created the disruption.

Halfway through fifth grade, I received an unexpected phone call that changed our lives forever.

"Hello, Mrs. Kaufman. This is Sam's teacher. There's something I want to ask you."

I froze, anxious about what she was going to say next.

"As a teacher, I wouldn't normally call a parent to ask such a personal question like I'm about to ask you—but since you and I have developed a close relationship during the few months that Sam has been in my class, I hope you will be receptive to my input."

"Yes," I said, my heart racing, "of course. I agree—we have had many heart-to-heart conversations about Sam, so go ahead. Ask away."

"Okay, thanks." She cleared her throat. "My question is: are you sure that Sam doesn't have ADHD?"

With my heart racing and my curiosity heightened, I replied, "I'm only as sure as the doctors, teachers, therapists, and the specialist who recently tested her are, and so far, they have all determined that she does not. Why do you ask?"

"Well, actually, I have a son with ADHD, and I noticed that Sam is displaying many of the same symptoms in my classroom that he has—not following verbal instructions, speaking out without being called upon, and missing assignments, to name a few."

"Wow," I said, relieved to be talking to someone who had some idea where I was coming from. "I'm so glad to hear you say all of this because I feel the same way!"

As we continued to talk, I started to disregard the previous advice and diagnoses from others and began placing my confidence in this knowing mother and concerned teacher—and my own gut instincts—instead. By the time I hung up the phone, I sensed that a new door was about to open.

7

FROM RAGES TO RITALIN

AFTER PROCESSING MY CONVERSATION with Sam's fifth-grade teacher, I jumped into action—this time by tracking down the information for a local psychiatrist who had coauthored a book about ADHD.

I dialed Dr. Stein's number and spoke to the receptionist, who filled me in on the process, which would include sessions with the doctor for Sam, Barry, and me and comprehensive questionnaires that her teachers would need to fill out.

"This should take approximately four to six weeks to complete," she concluded. "Would you like to set up Sam's first appointment?"

"Yes," I said, "that sounds great."

"Fantastic! Let's find a few dates for Sam's other appointments as well, and yours too."

I tried not to get my hopes up. After all, every one of my previous attempts at finding out why Sam acted the way she did had failed to provide helpful guidance. But this time felt different. I couldn't help but feel a little excited.

I sat at the doctor's desk, my hands sweaty and my heart racing, waiting for her to join me.

We'd completed everything requested of us over the previous

few weeks—the appointments, the questionnaires—and now I was here to discover the verdict. Unfortunately, Barry wasn't able to get away from work, so I was there alone.

And that was the day that Dr. Stein walked in, sat down at her desk, looked at me, and said, "Of course, Sam has ADHD!"

Upon hearing this long-awaited diagnosis, I couldn't help but reflect on the last ten years of Sam's life. My emotions got the best of me, and I started to cry.

With a confused look on her face, Dr. Stein asked, "Mrs. Kaufman, are you okay?"

"After years of searching for answers, I'm relieved to finally have the name of a disability to attribute to Sam's behavior and to know that it's not my fault," I told her in a shaky voice. Holding back more tears, I admitted, "But I'm also extremely overwhelmed. I need time to process this new revelation."

Without acknowledging my feelings, she jumped right in. "Okay, but I think it will help if you start Sam on an ADHD medication called Adderall immediately. I will give you a prescription now, and you can have it filled on your way home."

At that point my mind went into overdrive. I wished Barry was there to help me make this monumental decision. Since I was on my own, I decided to direct my many questions to the doctor. "Before making this decision, can you tell me what the possible side effects are? How will the medicine affect her personality? Will Sam outgrow ADHD, or will she have to be on medication her entire life?"

I was surprised and caught off guard when my inquiries appeared to annoy the doctor, and so many of my questions went unanswered. But mostly I was extremely offended by her next comment.

"Mrs. Kaufman, please accept my recommendation—after all, I am the doctor here. Without a doubt, you should trust my judgment and start Sam on Adderall as soon as possible."

I was an emotional wreck by this point and was finding little comfort in what I perceived to be this doctor's arrogant and unsympathetic attitude. But I managed to pull myself together and end the conversation.

"Look, I need to process everything I learned today," I said firmly. "I don't think it will be a problem if I wait to make a decision about medication for a few more days. After all, I spent years trying to figure out what's wrong with Sam—what difference will a few more days make?"

Without waiting for an answer, I left the psychiatrist's office with no intention of filling the prescription yet. I was grateful to finally have received the diagnosis I suspected all along—but my next step would be to find someone more compassionate and understanding to guide us going forward.

Before moving on, I felt it was important to tell Dr. Stein how I felt about our last appointment. I'd found her behavior deeply upsetting, and I thought she should know that. So, a few days later, a bit nervous but knowing I needed to get these feelings off my chest, I picked up the phone and called her office.

When she answered, I could tell she was surprised to hear my voice, but she listened as I told her why I was calling.

"I want you to know how uncomfortable I was in your office the other day," I said, trying to infuse more confidence into my tone than I was feeling. "I felt that you belittled my concerns and ignored my feelings. I know I asked a lot of questions, but that was so I could learn more about ADHD and the medication you prescribed. I was looking for you to help me make an educated and confident decision about Sam's treatment, not to question your intelligence—which is what you seemed to insinuate when you asked me to trust you because you are 'the doctor.' Intellectually, I know that putting Sam on medication is the right thing to do, as you suggested. I just needed to wait for my heart to catch up with my brain."

To my surprise, she seemed to hear what I was saying.

"I'm sorry," she said. "I didn't mean to say, 'I'm the doctor,' in a condescending way. I get excited when I find a child I think I can help and whom I feel will benefit from medication. Given my professional experience, I strongly suggested that you not wait. When I realized you were upset in my office, I thought I tried to help, but looking back, I can acknowledge that I wasn't very effective. I typically try to be a doctor who takes everything into consideration when making recommendations, and, in hindsight, I admit that I should have considered your feelings—those of a concerned mother—given the emotional state you were in. I recognize that in our situation, I overlooked this important factor."

I appreciated her apology and was grateful to her for making this long-awaited diagnosis, but it was clear to me that Dr. Stein's bedside manner fell short of my high expectations. I didn't feel I could fully trust in her advice or judgment going forward. So, although I felt better after our conversation, I decided I would move on to someone new, as planned.

I called our pediatrician, Dr. Cohen, for advice the next morning. After filling her in on Sam's diagnosis and my experience with Dr. Stein, I asked for her advice.

"I'm sorry to hear what happened," she said, "but you've called the right place. I think we can definitely help you make decisions about Sam's treatment. I'm not sure if you know that one of the doctors in our office specializes in ADHD. I'm confident that Dr. White will be able to help you learn more about the disorder, figure out which medication Sam should be taking, and guide you on how to proceed with therapy."

Feeling tremendously relieved, I made an appointment for the following week. Although I knew the road ahead would be a long one, I hung up the phone, this time feeling confident that I was in good hands and finally heading in the right direction.

I recently stumbled upon a blog written by Denis Asselin, a father whose son took his own life after struggling with body dysmorphic disorder for many years. In his heartfelt journal, *Walking With Nathaniel*, Denis wrote something that touched my own heart—and resonated loud and clear:

> *There's integrity in every child's illness (disability). The challenge is to respond accordingly and gently, and to realize that both child and parents are terrified.*

My sentiments exactly.

After my unsettling experience at Sam's diagnosis appointment, I wanted to be prepared for my first meeting with the new doctor, so I purchased lots of books and found as many articles about ADHD as I could. As I conducted my research, I discovered what I believe to be the most important fact a parent should know about ADHD: it is a neurobiological disability that is caused by a part of the brain that doesn't function as it should.

This discovery was so incredibly validating for me. It reaffirmed what I'd always believed to be the case. My daughter's outrageous behavior was not my fault, and—something that is not easy for most people to understand—it wasn't *Sam's* fault, either! This revelation fueled my inner strength and self-confidence and gave me permission to practice self-compassion as I moved forward. With this important bit of information embedded in my mind, I also found myself getting less angry at Sam's outbursts and better able to focus on helping my child and healing our family relationships.

I also learned from my research that most children with ADHD have a parent with the same disability. After reading the symptoms of adult ADHD, I was astonished to find myself recognizing many of my own shortcomings—being unorganized, forgetful, and easily distracted, to name a few. This unexpected discovery (which, much later, would be confirmed by a therapist) not only answered questions I had about challenges I was facing in my own life but also helped me to better appreciate my daughter's difficulties.

In light of my own diagnosis, one might say that it actually *was* my fault that Sam acted the way she did. After all, given everything I have read about the hereditary nature of ADHD, there is no doubt that I am the genetic source of Sam's disability. That is something I have learned to accept but not dwell upon since, unfortunately, I had no control over Sam's misfortune in inheriting this disability.

By the time I was done reading up on ADHD, I was certain that Sam's lack of self-control, impulsivity, and severe behavior problems had not developed because of my own so-called "inadequacies." It was now clear to me, beyond the shadow of a doubt, that her inappropriate and outrageous behaviors were symptoms of ADHD.

Even better? I learned that ADHD was treatable. But there was no one path. There were lots of medication choices, and each one had various pros and cons. I wanted to learn as much as possible about all of them before meeting with the new doctor. I planned on going into this next appointment with extensive research under my belt and my eyes wide open.

Dr. White, the ADHD specialist at our pediatrician's office, was personable and kind. The moment we started talking, I felt completely at ease.

"I understand Sam was diagnosed with ADHD, and you are looking for guidance regarding medication," she said gently. "Can you tell me a little bit about Sam so I can get an idea of where we should start?"

"Yes, thank you!" I said eagerly. "Sam is ten years old, and it's taken us years to finally figure out why she has been acting out, fighting with her sister, and throwing temper tantrums over insignificant issues, among other things. Other doctors, therapists, and teachers all determined she did not have ADHD until the most recent evaluation. Unfortunately, I didn't feel comfortable with the psychiatrist who made the diagnosis, so I reached out to Sam's pediatrician, Dr. Cohen, and she led me to you."

After a lengthy discussion with the doctor, we decided to start Sam on Adderall, as Dr. Stein had suggested. But unlike Dr. Stein, Dr. White took the time to explain to me why she thought it was the best fit for Sam. It worked for many kids, and she felt the side effects were not as intense as those of the other medications she might have prescribed, so she thought it best to try it first.

Reassured by our conversation, I left Dr. White's office feeling more confident than ever before—and less emotional too. This time, I went directly to the pharmacy and filled the prescription.

We learned fairly soon that Adderall was not the right medication for Sam. Not long after starting the pills, she became extremely lethargic and moody.

I called Dr. White to let her know, and after evaluating the symptoms, she switched Sam to Ritalin. Disappointed but not losing hope, I jumped into the car and, once again, drove to the drugstore to fill the new prescription.

Because Sam had experienced a negative reaction to the first drug, I kept my expectations in check when she started taking Ritalin—but I didn't have to do so for long. I noticed a dramatic improvement in her demeanor almost immediately. For me, this remarkable change in behavior confirmed the ADHD diagnosis and gave me a glimpse of hope for the future.

Prior to putting Sam on medication, taking her shopping for shoes was one of my worst nightmares. Inevitably, she would find a pair that she loved, but nine out of ten times, they would be the wrong size or inappropriate for what she needed. When this happened, she would start to cry and insist on buying the wrong size or style anyway. I always felt embarrassed when I had to deal with situations like this in public.

When I realized that Sam needed a new pair of shoes just before Thanksgiving that year, I tried not to panic. She had started on Ritalin a few weeks earlier, and I felt cautiously optimistic as she took her afternoon pill and we headed out the door.

Feeling nervous and trying not to expect too much from the medication, I took a deep breath as we walked into the store.

Soon after our arrival, I felt a familiar angst as I watched Sam eye a pair of shoes.

"Hey, Mom, what about these?" she said. "Can you see if they have my size?"

I crossed my fingers and found a salesperson to help. "Can you see if you have these shoes in a size three, please?"

Sam and I waited for her to come back. When she returned empty-handed a minute later, I braced myself for the outburst that typically followed—but instead, I heard Sam say, "That's okay. Let's try somewhere else, Mom." Then I watched her quietly walk out of the store.

For a moment I just stood there in complete disbelief. Then I followed her outside. When I caught up to Sam at the car, she saw the tears welling up in my eyes.

Her forehead crinkled in confusion. "Are you okay, Mom?"

"Do you understand what just happened?" I asked, my voice quivering. "I am so proud of the calm way you handled yourself when they didn't have your size!"

She smiled at me. "It's not a big deal. If we can't find the shoes at another store, I'll pick something different."

To some this might seem like a non-event, but to me, it was *huge*. At that moment, I knew in my heart that Sam was going to make it and that ADHD was indeed the core reason for many of her inappropriate behaviors. I didn't know at the time that the following eleven years would continue to be a tremendous challenge for Sam, but in many of the hardest moments, I would look back on that experience and be reminded of the long-lost hope I regained that day.

We arrived at Barry's cousin Nancy's house for Thanksgiving that year with great anticipation. Up until that day, it was hard to remember a prior holiday gathering without some disturbance from Sam. Not liking where she was seated at the table, not wanting to eat what was being served, or wanting to watch TV instead of visiting with family members would typically push Sam over the edge and result in a temper tantrum—exactly what had happened a few years earlier at Thanksgiving in NYC. With the positive shoe-shopping experience behind us, I felt confident that this year would be better, but I decided not to tell anyone in our extended family that Sam had started taking Ritalin. I wanted to see what their unbiased reaction would be. Thanksgiving would be our first test case.

Needless to say, I was guarded when we first arrived, but shortly after we sat down to eat, my heart filled with joy as I watched my well-behaved daughter interacting with our relatives like never before.

I listened as Nancy started the conversation: "Hi, Sam, how's school going?"

"Well, I don't usually love school, but lately, I like it much better than last year," Sam replied honestly. "I really like my teacher, and I have some friends in my class, so that makes it fun. I'm also getting pretty good grades so far, so nothing to complain about."

Sam sat through the rest of the meal—eating what was offered, chatting with everyone, and, for the first time ever, appearing to enjoy herself.

The following morning, I received two phone calls—one from my father and another from Barry's cousin—telling me what a dramatic improvement they'd noticed in Sam's behavior and commenting on how much she had matured. I thanked them for noticing but decided to delay telling anyone about the medication for a bit longer. Sam rarely received praise for her behavior, and I wanted to bask in these accolades for a while and savor the feeling of having witnessed this epic moment in her life.

So, here's what I learned about ADHD medications early on: First of all, there's no way of knowing exactly which brand and what dose will be the most effective and long-lasting or if your child will experience any of the side effects listed on the insert. Unfortunately, ADHD is not like many other medical conditions, where a blood test can guide doctors to the optimal dosage with reasonable accuracy. This means that it can be extremely confusing for parents and challenging for doctors when deciding on which drug to use, how many milligrams to prescribe, and whether to try brand or generic formulas and regular or sustained-release pills. Even more frustrating is that once you find a drug that seems to be working—like Ritalin at the beginning of Sam's ADHD medication saga—there are many variables that can change over time, making it necessary to reevaluate and, ultimately, make a switch. Believe it or not, we changed Sam's medication seven or eight times over the years before going full circle and eventually ending up with Adderall, the medication she'd tried in the first place.

As for the side effects—they can seem really scary. When I first read the long list of possible side effects of Ritalin, I was shocked. Would I be committing child abuse by allowing my ten-year-old to ingest pills with such serious warnings? I wondered who in their right mind would subject their child to such a risk—yet I also knew that Ritalin was widely used in the United States to treat ADHD.

What is a mother to do when her child is suffering and the recommendation from well-respected doctors is to put her on a drug with an insert containing the following glaring warnings (some of which I had to use a dictionary to decipher the meaning of)?

> *ADVERSE REACTIONS: Nervousness and insomnia . . .*
> *hypersensitivity (including skin rash . . . dermatitis. . . .) . . .*
> *anorexia; nausea; dizziness; palpitations; headache; drows-*
> *iness; blood pressure and pulse changes . . . tachycardia;*
> *angina; cardiac arrhythmia; abdominal pain; weight loss . . .*
> *Tourette's syndrome . . . Toxic psychosis . . . abnormal liver*
> *function, ranging from transaminase elevation to hepatic*
> *coma . . . cerebral arteritis and/or occlusion; leukopenia and/*
> *or anemia; transient depressed mood . . . scalp hair loss . . .*
> *neuroleptic malignant syndrome (NMS). . . . In children, loss of*
> *appetite, abdominal pain, weight loss during prolonged ther-*
> *apy, insomnia, and tachycardia may occur more frequently;*
> *however, any of the other adverse reactions listed above may*
> *also occur.*

Although conflicted about my decision, I, like millions of other parents, weighed the pros and cons, decided to accept the risks, and filled the prescription. But as I anxiously gave Sam her first pill, the warnings on the medication's insert were very much on my mind. From that decision on, I took my job as Sam's protector more seriously than ever before and made it my responsibility to monitor her progress and evaluate the side effects thereafter—starting with that first trial with Adderall. She became lethargic and moody after taking it for just a few days. Because I had spent so much time staring at that "Adverse Reactions" warning, I immediately remembered that drowsiness and depression were listed as possible adverse reactions, so I called Dr. White and requested that we try something else.

Over the next ten years, Sam did experience many of the documented side effects (insomnia, loss of appetite, abdominal pain, weight loss, heart palpitations, and moodiness) of the medications she took, but I can safely say that they never appeared serious enough to cause alarm or make us consider having her stop taking ADHD medication altogether. At times, we changed the dosage or switched medications, but overall, we—Sam's family, her doctors, teachers, therapists, camp counselors, and friends—believed that the benefits definitely outweighed the side effects.

If you were to ask Sam whether *she* thought the same—well, I know now she would disagree. Unfortunately, I didn't find out how she felt about the medications until much later in life.

The first summer after Sam's diagnosis, she and Dana went to sleep-away camp together—and Sam immediately began to butt heads with the camp director. She had little experience with children like Sam or training for dealing with a child with ADHD, and her solution was to lose her patience and yell at Sam every time she challenged her.

Sam felt embarrassed that she had to go to the nurse every day for her medication, and that was a big point of contention between her and the director. After having one too many arguments with Sam about this, the director called me to complain.

After listening to her ramble on about how bad she thought my daughter was for a few minutes, I jumped right in. "It sounds like you and Sam are having a tough time seeing eye to eye," I said. "Would it be possible to put Laurie"—the division head who liked Sam and who Sam liked and respected back— "in charge of her medication and overall activities?"

"I guess we could try that," the director acquiesced.

This turned out to be a lifesaver for Sam. Things improved drastically after that, and she went on to spend five more great summers at that camp in the years to come. This was a wonderful outcome for a number of reasons, not least of which was that summers together at sleepaway camp played an important role in helping Dana and Sam mend their often-turbulent relationship. The bond they developed while being away from Barry and me was an unexpected byproduct I could never have imagined when we first decided to let Sam go a year after Dana started. I later learned that Dana was there to comfort Sam when the director yelled at her or punished her by taking away a privilege she was looking forward to, and it brought the girls closer together than they had ever been before. It didn't solve all their problems, of course, but it did give them a foundation that helped them survive those teenage years when their differences seemed so vast and their arguments so bitter.

I have a feeling that if Dana had continued to write in her diary during these years, her entries would have portrayed a much brighter picture of her feelings about her younger sister.

8

504 IS MORE THAN JUST A NUMBER

"INCLUDED IN SAM'S 504 PLAN are provisions for an extra set of books to be kept at home, a daily assignment sheet to be checked by her teachers, copies of weekly class notes, study sheets for exam preparation, extended time on tests, informing us about upcoming assignments and tests, and seating Sam near the teacher," Sam's guidance counselor explained as we sat together in a classroom at Sam's school.

It hadn't been long since Sam's diagnosis of ADHD, and we were meeting for the first time with her fifth-grade teachers and a group of school administrators to set a plan into motion for the following year.

As usual, I'd done my homework before we met. I'd learned as much as I could about a federal law that requires public schools to provide classroom accommodations and modifications to students with disabilities who do not qualify for special education services (which Sam did not) and was pleased to discover that the list of eligible disabilities included ADHD. It didn't take long for me to familiarize myself with this law, referred to as "Section 504," and soon after become Sam's biggest advocate.

At this first meeting, we reviewed Sam's academic, medical, and social history and came up with a comprehensive plan that gave us high hopes for her educational future. I was surprised by, but on board with, all of the modifications being offered. On paper, it appeared that Sam would be given the accommodations she needed to succeed at school.

What I soon came to realize, however, was that the prescription for Sam's success had little to do with the piece of paper authorizing her plan and more to do with her teachers' willingness to adhere to the provisions, their experience with and understanding of ADHD, and their ability to accept the diagnosis in the first place.

I understand how difficult it is for teachers to have a student like Sam in their classroom. I know firsthand that controlling impulsivity, distractibility, and oppositional behavior can be a near-impossible task one-on-one, so I can imagine how hard it must be for teachers to deal with these ADHD traits in a room full of students with a wide range of needs. That's why I listened to Sam's teachers with a sympathetic ear and a positive attitude and generally supported their decisions—as long as I felt confident that they were making those decisions with her best interests in mind. I wasn't shy in speaking up, however, when I felt they were acting without regard to her disability or her 504 Plan.

What I came to understand was that the teachers who had a positive influence on Sam were few and far between. Unfortunately, most of the educators she came into contact with had limited training in dealing with ADHD symptoms in the classroom and lacked the tools needed to help Sam succeed. On top of that, not all teachers and administrators realize what an impressionable and long-lasting effect they have on students and their families, especially those suffering from a disability such as ADHD.

Sam once told me that she thinks public schools in America are designed in a way that inherently does not work for students with ADHD. Reflecting on her turbulent academic career and the frustration I experienced while helping her navigate that system, I have to agree with my daughter. The phrase "swimming against the tide" comes to mind when I painfully recall the innumerable meetings with teachers, principals, and guidance counselors, the daily fights over homework, and the tears of anger and self-doubt—mine and hers—that typically followed.

When Sam entered sixth grade, I wasn't exactly sure what to expect. From my perspective, the accommodations provided in her 504 Plan seemed reasonable for her teachers to implement. What I wasn't so sure about was how they would handle Sam's distracted and impulsive behavior now that these problems were documented as manifestations of a disability.

During this time, I read—and it made complete sense to me—that teachers should handle issues like ADHD symptoms with extreme sensitivity and should not attribute inconsistent or inferior performance as a sign of laziness, lack of motivation, or lesser intelligence. I also learned that holding students with ADHD to the same standards and classroom rules as other students or punishing them for calling out or displaying what some might consider disrespectful behavior is frowned upon by those who are trained in this area. Rather, teachers are encouraged to talk to the student in private when issues arise, praise positive behavior, and, by all means, avoid criticism or sarcasm.

Without these intangible expectations written into Sam's plan, I silently questioned how she would fare given the lack of special training provided to teachers in our district. With my research filed away for future reference and Sam's classroom accommodations set into motion, I still tried to keep a positive outlook as Sam began her first year of middle school as a student with a documented disability who would be receiving provisions under federal Section 504. It was unnerving, to say the least.

I let out part of the breath I'd been holding in when Sam received her sixth-grade team assignment the summer before she entered middle school. I was relieved to learn that her math teacher had previously been a special education instructor and was part of the team that created Sam's 504 Plan for that year, and another teacher—one of Dana's favorites when she was in middle school—had an approach to classroom learning that I felt would be a perfect fit for Sam. Maybe this new plan would work after all.

One day, early that fall of her first year in middle school, Sam came home and told me that her social studies teacher—the one Dana had loved—had taken her shoe away during class.

Her shoe!? Sam didn't seem upset about it, but it was a strange thing for a teacher to do, so I made an appointment with her teacher to get a better sense of why it had happened.

I got straight to the point. "I came in to see you because Sam came home earlier this week and told me you had taken her shoe from her during class. I was wondering why?"

With a smile on her face, the teacher explained, "Sam has a habit of losing her pencils and typically shows up for class without a writing utensil. Instead of punishing her by making her sit in class without taking notes like some other teachers might do, I made a deal with her. I gave Sam a pencil in return for one of her shoes. I know this is an unorthodox approach, but it assured me that she would return the pencil before walking out of the classroom at the end of the period. I was also hoping the experience might prompt her to remember to bring something to write with the next time."

"And how did Sam react to that?" I asked.

She chuckled. "She was a really good sport about it, actually."

I shook my head, grinning. "Unorthodox indeed, but genius too! I love it." I wished all of Sam's teachers were so willing to come up with creative solutions to address her challenges.

During that year, I reached out to this teacher for more than just academic advice. When Sam was having typical pre-teen difficulties with some of her girlfriends, I asked for her impartial opinion since I was feeling emotional and too close to the situation.

After hearing what I had to say, she thought for a minute, then said, "I want you to know that I would rather have ten students like Sam in my class than one who exhibits mean and vindictive traits that often materialize in young girls her age." She leaned forward in her seat and continued. "From my perspective, Sam is a warm, caring child with a big heart. Yes, she may do some things that come across as mean-spirited due to her impulsive behavior, but she is not by nature a mean person."

I left the classroom that day in high spirits, similar to how I'd felt after our shoe discussion, and I held this conversation in the back of my mind forever after. In the years to come, I would often find it comforting to recall her kind words—especially when confronted by others who questioned Sam's integrity and had a completely different perspective about my daughter.

Sam's math class posed a different type of problem that year. It was held during the dreaded period right after lunch, a time when she would arrive at class preoccupied with just having seen her friends and distracted by the social issues of the day. Luckily, her math teacher was one of the educators who had helped create Sam's 504 Plan and had experience teaching students with ADHD, so she was ready, willing, and able to deal with whatever Sam threw her way. What impressed me the most about her intuitive teaching techniques was her ability to foresee a problem and her ingenuity in finding ways to eliminate the triggers before Sam had a chance to pull them.

Case in point: when Sam would barge into class after lunch, all hyped up from being with her friends, her teacher would pull her aside and whisper in her ear, "Sam, I want you to go back out of the room for two minutes. Go to the bathroom or run up and down the hall. Anything to 'shake your sillies out.' When you get back, I want you ready to pay attention and be ready to work."

It was a simple idea—but so effective! Upon her return, Sam was typically better prepared to participate with the rest of the class. I'm sure there were days when this technique was not as effective as it was with others. However, Sam responded positively to this teacher, who showed respect for her disability and made efforts to create an atmosphere that was conducive to helping students like Sam thrive in the classroom in spite of their limitations.

As Sam successfully wrapped up sixth grade, I allowed myself to hold high hopes for the next year and those that followed. But it wouldn't be long before I realized that these two teachers were exceptions to the norm in our district—and our true uphill struggle was about to begin.

One day, not long after her seventh-grade school year began, Sam came home visibly upset and told me, "Mrs. Baker asked me in front of the entire class today if I had taken my medicine this morning!"

My mouth dropped open. "What!?"

My shock quickly gave way to anger. When Barry and I had met with the 504 team before Sam entered middle school, we'd been assured that our discussions and the fact that Sam took medication would be kept confidential. In our minds, this meant that teachers would not address ADHD issues with Sam or us in front of others and would not discuss confidential information with anyone outside of our 504 team. We felt confident that her teachers would respect this trust and never suspected that they would purposefully use Sam's disability against her. Clearly, our confidence had been misplaced.

I understood how easy it was for Sam to get under her teachers' skin and what a challenge it must be for them to manage the symptoms of her disability in the classroom, so I tried not to jump to conclusions. Maybe Sam had just pushed things too far that morning, causing Mrs. Baker to lose her patience momentarily and say something she probably regretted.

I did some digging. What I soon learned was that this particular teacher was constantly reprimanding and belittling Sam in front of the class for not paying attention, fidgeting at her desk, and calling out—all classic symptoms of ADHD. All of Sam's sixth-grade teachers had managed not to lash out at her. Why couldn't this teacher do the same?

Though furious about Mrs. Baker's breach of Sam's privacy, Barry and I were also nervous about jeopardizing Sam's grade in her class, so we decided to wait until the end of the year to address it head-on.

What I discovered about 504 accommodations in our district that year was the problem they posed for some teachers outside of the core team of math, science, social studies, and language arts. When three of Sam's seventh-grade electives teachers called me during the year to complain about her behavior in their classroom, I knew there must have been a disconnect somewhere along the line.

After speaking to those teachers, I was shocked. One teacher's problems with Sam were clearly due to a lack of knowledge about ADHD and how to help students who display overt symptoms. The other two had never even received a copy of Sam's 504 Plan at the beginning of the year! I was quite disturbed when I discovered that they had no idea that Sam had a disability.

I received the first call in October, just two months into the school year. After hearing the teacher's long list of complaints, I was taken aback.

"Do you have a copy of Sam's 504 plan?" I asked her in a confused tone.

"Yes, Mrs. Kaufman, I do have a copy, but that's no excuse for Sam talking too much and not listening when I speak," she insisted. "She misses instructions and often calls out and interrupts. It is difficult to determine if it's ADHD or if Sam is just too social. I'm worried that it might be more complex. I'm puzzled because sometimes Sam gets it immediately when I explain a concept one-on-one, but other times she just . . . *doesn't.*"

After processing her barrage of concerns, I began the first of what would turn out to be many "information sessions" to come with this teacher. I began by explaining, "I want you to know that everything you are complaining about happens to mirror the most common symptoms of ADHD. If you look at her 504 Plan, it should include some techniques you can use to avoid situations that you are experiencing with Sam. If not, I can offer suggestions to help you defuse the disruptions. And by the way, where do you have Sam sitting in the classroom?"

"She's in the fourth row back, near one of her best friends."

Well, no wonder, I thought. "Are you aware that Sam's 504 Plan requires her to be seated in the front near the teacher?"

"Yes," she said, "but Sam didn't want to sit there. I guess I'll try to move her if you think that might help."

I realized rather quickly that the issue here was an unnerved teacher who questioned Sam's diagnosis and expected her to perform like the rest of the students in her classroom in spite of her disability. Unfortunately, these kinds of situations—teachers having unrealistic expectations of Sam and failing to follow through on the requirements of her 504 Plan as a result—occurred often throughout her school years. Soon, this would become the main focus of my advocacy for my struggling daughter.

"Hi, Mrs. Kaufman, this is Mr. Davis. I'm Sam's teacher in one of her elective classes. I'm having problems with Sam not paying attention and not following instructions as needed. I thought you should know that her reputation of being a 'bad kid' proceeded her and that some of her previous teachers warned me that she is way too social in class."

I almost dropped the phone as Mr. Davis admitted all of this to me. I was stunned that he didn't seem to have any qualms saying these things to the mother of the child in question. It was troubling to learn that behind the scenes, some of Sam's previous teachers were jeopardizing her academic success by labeling her a "bad kid" and singling her out before she even had a chance to step up to the plate.

Finding it hard to control my anger, I took a deep breath and asked, "Are you aware that Sam has ADHD? Do you have a copy of her 504 Plan? I hope that you are using some of the required techniques provided to help Sam succeed in your classroom rather than relying on what you heard about her from other teachers."

Sounding a bit apologetic, he replied, "Um, well, to be honest, I was not given a copy of Sam's 504 Plan. I was not aware that she has ADHD. I guess that could be contributing to the problem."

With a sigh, I went on, for the second time in just a few months, to describe the symptoms of ADHD, make sure he received a copy of Sam's 504 Plan, and offer suggestions on how to help Sam succeed in his classroom, regardless of what other teachers might have said about her. I didn't go a step further and address the confidentiality lines that may have been crossed by whichever of Sam's middle school teachers gossiped about her, and to this day, I am disappointed in myself for that. At the time, though, my only focus was on attempting to salvage her relationship with her current teachers in the hopes that they would do better than their predecessors.

The pattern continued when I received yet a third call from Sam's Physical Education teacher, Ms. Jordan. This time, to my relief, she was looking to me for advice, not to simply complain about my daughter. Since she, too, was unaware of Sam's 504 Plan, I once again described the symptoms of ADHD and made clear to her how Sam reacted when she was put on the defensive.

"There are much better ways to get through to her than putting her on the spot," I explained.

It was a productive conversation, and I planned to talk to Sam about it when I found a good time—but before I had a chance, something unexpected happened: Ms. Jordan called me again a few days later.

"Hi, Mrs. Kaufman, it's me again," she said. "I want you to know what happened after school recently."

Here we go, I thought, bracing myself for the unknown.

"I was with my son at the middle school baseball game," Ms. Jordan said, "and we ran into Sam there. She and my son talked and laughed together throughout the game—and as I watched their interaction, I was able to see through Sam's often rough exterior and discover a kind and engaging child underneath."

I couldn't have been more pleased to hear those kind words. "Oh, wow, she didn't mention that she saw you and your son at the game. Thank you so much for letting me know and for acknowledging the positive side of Sam you experienced."

"You're welcome—but there's more," she said. "Shortly after our chance meeting, Sam and I discovered that we both watch a popular television show, *90210*, and we started to discuss the previous night's episode at school the day after it was on. I have to admit, I have noticed a positive change in Sam since then."

Yes! I thought. *Bingo.* "When Sam senses that a teacher is not trying to change her or make her act like the other students who don't have a disability, she begins to develop a positive attitude toward her teacher and toward learning in general," I explained enthusiastically. "She ends up becoming more respectful and, ultimately, changes her behavior, which helps her teachers become more effective educators for her."

In the years that followed, I often shared this example of a successful, although unplanned, way to reach Sam with other instructors who struggled with her unruly behavior and looked to me for advice. Those who listened and put in the effort to make a similar connection often managed to develop a much better relationship with Sam than those who didn't.

As Sam's seventh-grade year drew to an end, it was clear to me that the many discussions I'd had with Mrs. Baker, the teacher who'd asked Sam if she'd taken her medication that morning, as well as with the administration, had been totally ineffective. From my perspective, the issues I brought up were disregarded entirely, and some of the provisions in Sam's written plan were still being ignored by many of her teachers as well. After final grades were posted, with our frustrations running high, we arranged for a meeting with Mrs. Baker and the principal.

At first, as we reiterated our concerns about the teacher's treatment of Sam throughout the year, she showed little contrition. Then Barry changed into his "lawyer voice" and asked, "Did you or did you not ask Sam, in front of the entire class, if she had taken her medicine one day?"

Suddenly, looking a bit nervous, Mrs. Baker nodded yes.

"I need you to know that doing this in front of the other students has destroyed our trust in you," Barry said, "and that divulging confidential information from Sam's 504 Plan is unconscionable and inexcusable." We all knew that what she had done could be grounds for a lawsuit, though neither Barry nor I said that out loud.

It was only then that we finally saw signs of Mrs. Baker understanding why we were so concerned. With tears in her eyes—though we were not sure if they were from fear of losing her job or remorse for what she had done—she said haltingly, "I never meant to hurt Sam. I like your daughter, and my intentions were always to try and help her."

We were not convinced, and regardless, it was too late for her to do anything differently with Sam since the school year was over. But we did hope that what transpired in that meeting might at least benefit other students to come.

9

RIDING THE ROLLER COASTER

BY THE TIME SAM REACHED eighth grade, my high hopes for her 504 Plan being the ticket to her success in school had been severely deflated. Even with classroom accommodations in place, many of Sam's teachers continued to ignore some of the provisions and often expected her to fit into the cookie-cutter mold of a "typical" student without ADHD. It was now clear to me that a 504 Plan was not the cure-all I'd anticipated it might be. With high school just around the corner, advocating for my daughter was more important than it had ever been.

Sam came home from school one day and burst into tears for no apparent reason. Concerned and confused by the sudden change in her demeanor, I sat her down on the couch and asked gently, "Hey, Sammy, why the tears?"

Through her sobbing, she blurted out, "I hate myself! I'm ugly and I wish I were dead."

Holding back tears of my own, I took her into my arms and tried to calm her down. This episode left me anxious about what Sam might do to herself if this apparent depression were to go untreated. I immediately reached out to friends and our pediatrician for a new therapist recommendation and landed on one who came highly recommended. I made an appointment, hoping desperately that she would finally be a good fit for Sam and our entire family.

In the beginning, Sam responded fairly well to Dr. Rosen. Although she didn't feel a close connection with her, she went to sessions willingly and began to show signs of improvement. I met with Dr. Rosen on my own after Sam had seen her a couple of times. She reassured me that she agreed with our pediatrician's previous assessment of Sam: She was hurting inside, but she did not see signs of a child who would intentionally hurt herself. Hearing this was a huge relief, given some of the disturbing things I'd heard Sam say about herself, and it gave me the confidence to move on to other concerns.

During our private sessions, the therapist listened to my frustrations about Sam and our volatile family dynamics. She offered advice and suggestions, but I soon discovered that this board-certified, licensed psychologist disagreed with my premise that Sam's behavior problems were overt symptoms of a disability. I was confused when, a year after we began meeting with the doctor, she started one of our sessions differently from how she'd started all of the others. "So, I've been thinking that you shouldn't use ADHD as an excuse for Sam's inappropriate behavior," she announced. "I feel like that's a cop-out for some of the things you might be doing to contribute to Sam's problems. I actually think that you helped create a monster!"

I was stunned by her words—so much so that I was essentially speechless. I must have said something between that comment and leaving her office, but everything following that moment was a blur. I was horrified that this trained psychotherapist verbalized such a hurtful allegation, especially at a time when I was so clearly feeling extremely vulnerable and desperate for help.

That day I wrote the letter I included in the preface of this book. Although I ended my note by saying, "*I want you to know that I am writing this letter to help Sam, not to alleviate my own discomfort*

because you are blaming me for her problems," that wasn't *entirely*
true. My primary goal was to help Sam, but I also wanted Dr. Rosen
to understand how hurtful her accusations were so that in the future,
she might think twice before making similar comments to other parents seeking her help and advice.

I had thought that Sam's ADHD diagnosis would dissuade my
biggest critics (including my husband, at times) from blaming me for
my daughter's problems—making them less judgmental and more
understanding of my struggles. Turned out I was very wrong.

Ever since learning about the classroom accommodations being
offered to Sam, Barry and I met with her 504 team at the beginning
of each school year to set her plan into motion and then again in May
to brainstorm for the following year. Most of the meetings were very
productive—but the one with Sam's teachers at the end of eighth grade
was far from it. Frustrating and even mind-boggling, this meeting was
a clear example of how unprepared many teachers in our district were
for dealing with students struggling with ADHD or other challenges.

Barry wasn't able to make it this time, so I went alone to meet
with most of Sam's eighth-grade teachers, her guidance counselor,
and the principal of the middle school. The principal began the meeting by asking each teacher to report on Sam's progress throughout
the year. I sat quietly and listened.

"Sam continues to be easily distracted and fidgets in her seat a
lot," one teacher began. "She is very social in class, which often causes
a disruption."

"Sam's assignments are often late," another teacher chimed in,
"and she needs me to review what needs to be done before she leaves."

Only one teacher had anything positive to say about Sam. With
a smile on her face, she said Sam was very well-behaved in her classroom and enjoyable to have as a student.

I was completely caught off guard by the other teachers'

complaints. Everything they were saying was a textbook description of the symptoms of ADHD—information that was clearly outlined in her 504 Plan. I forced myself not to react since the principal had expressed a desire for all of the teachers to report before we began our discussion.

Next, it was Sam's English teacher's turn to speak. She had thirty years of teaching experience, so I hoped she would see things differently and change the tone of the meeting.

"Well, Mrs. Kaufman," she began slowly, "I'm wondering if Sam might need glasses. I notice that she doesn't follow along when someone in the back of the room is reading out loud."

At this point, I couldn't contain myself any longer. I had to interrupt. "Can I say a few things before anyone else jumps in?" I asked loudly, eyes on the principal.

"Of course, Mrs. Kaufman," he said.

I composed myself for a moment, then looked around the table at each teacher before saying, "I'm confused by many of your complaints. Aren't all of you aware of why we are at this meeting in the first place? Don't you know that Sam has ADHD? All of the things you are reporting as problems are common symptoms of her disability, which suggests to me that maybe you haven't read Sam's 504 Plan—you know, the one that was given to you at the beginning of the school year?"

Before they had a chance to respond, I asked a room-silencing question: "What are each of you doing to help Sam succeed in your classroom?"

No one had an answer for me.

Looking a bit uncomfortable, the principal asked me—a non-educator— "What would you suggest?"

Without hesitation, I reached into my bag and pulled out a document titled "504 Accommodation Considerations." I tried to come to these meetings well-prepared.

"Since I can't be in the classroom to help," I said, "you might want to implement some of the accommodations listed in this document. Included are approximately seventy-five suggestions for teachers to consider in the following areas:

Physical Arrangement of Room (stand near student when giving instructions, avoid sitting student near distracting stimuli); Lesson Presentation (write key points on board, make sure directions are understood); Assignments/Worksheets (give extra time, break work into smaller segments); Test Taking (allow open book exams, give exam orally); Organization (assign homework buddy, develop reward system); Behaviors (praise specific behaviors, ignore inappropriate behavior if possible, allow student time out of seat to run errands); Special Considerations (attend in-service training, suggest parenting programs)."

Hopeful that this group would be receptive to my input, I'd brought extra copies of the list with me. But my heart sank when the only teacher who stopped to take one on her way out was the one who had not complained about Sam's behavior at the beginning of the meeting. The others didn't care enough to even take a copy and *act* as if they were willing to try something new. Instead, they belittled my concerns by walking away empty-handed.

Disheartened by this blatant lack of interest in my child's success in the classroom, I left the meeting feeling defeated with low expectations for what was to come for Sam in high school.

In light of my discouraging experiences at Sam's middle school, I reached out to the Director of Guidance at the high school right at the beginning of ninth grade, wanting to help Sam begin her new school on the right foot.

At our meeting, I emphasized the importance of Sam's teachers being made aware of her disability and receiving a copy of the required accommodations spelled out in her 504 Plan. I also described some of the behaviors to look out for and best practices for dealing with her conduct in the classroom.

"Please explain to her teachers that Sam is very forgetful, gets distracted easily, doesn't always write down her assignments, and is very chatty," I said. "Knowing that these are symptoms of ADHD and not intentional acts of misbehavior may help them to understand her better. In the past, Sam's teachers have found her to be very responsive to positive reinforcement and encouragement rather than criticism and punishment when they needed her to change a behavior or perform better academically."

I was pleased that the director was receptive to my input and promised to inform Sam's teachers about her 504 Plan and my suggestions. With guarded hopes, I held my breath and crossed my fingers that Sam would find the last leg of her public school experiences less confrontational than the previous ones.

Even as we focused on improving Sam's experience at school, things at home weren't always going so well. Knowing how much she loved me didn't always help me stay in control, as I became the main target of her verbal attacks when things didn't go her way.

One day Sam came running out of her room yelling for me as if there were a big emergency—"Mom! MOM!!!"

Worried that something terrible had happened, I dropped everything and ran to her.

When she saw me, she blurted out, "Mommy, Mommy, I need you to drive me to a friend's house now. I told her you would take me, so let's go, okay?"

Relieved that something bad had not happened, I replied, "Sam, I'm in the middle of something. I'll take you in about fifteen minutes." I turned around to go back into my room.

"I WANT TO GO NOW!!!" Sam screamed. "I already told my friend I would be there soon!"

I realized early on how important it is for parents to have tremendous control over their own behavior when faced with defiant, out-of-control children. But sometimes, I just couldn't hold on, and I am embarrassed to admit that I often dropped to Sam's level. This was one of those occasions.

I turned around to face her—and lost it. "STOP YELLING AT ME," I shouted at her. "I WILL TAKE YOU WHEN I'M READY."

Instead of backing down, Sam started running toward me. I could see by the look in her eyes and the expression on her face that she had lost control, and my anger was only escalating the situation. Knowing I needed to physically remove myself from the situation, I locked myself in the bathroom—a common retreat for me.

My memories of sitting on the closed toilet seat as Sam continued to cry and scream at me from the other side of the door are haunting and brought up a myriad of emotions. I often chastise myself for my own lack of self-control, which is what led me to hide in the bathroom in the first place. But then I think that maybe I shouldn't be so hard on myself for having behaved so poorly. Instead, I should focus on the fact that I found a way to stop myself from doing or saying something that I would regret later on.

In hindsight, I realize that, once again, I was relying on my maternal instincts to protect my daughter. In these cases, however, I was protecting her from *me*—what a troubling thought.

During Sam's first year in high school, her grades started to drop, and she began having problems with some of her teachers and friends. At home, her behavior was worse than ever. We were at our wits' end.

To help turn things around academically, I hired tutors for Sam—and it worked better than anticipated! Her grades improved, she gained more confidence in her abilities, and, much to my relief, she was able to smooth things over with some of her teachers. Although she struggled with a few volatile friendships, she developed a new group of girlfriends who had a positive impact on her overall demeanor both in school and at home. I noticed a positive change in her relationship with Dana and less friction between the two of them now that they were both in high school together.

As for my relationship with Sam, in spite of what the therapist had said to me about having created a monster, I stayed true to myself and never gave up on my daughter. Eventually, she was able to pull herself out of her funk and move on to tenth grade with passing grades and a much better attitude—a positive momentum she maintained throughout the entire year.

Eleventh grade, however, posed new problems. With college lurking on the horizon, this was an important year academically, but academics seemed to be at the bottom of Sam's priority list. She was far more interested in the large social network she had developed. In hopes of trying to get Sam to refocus on her schoolwork, I wrote this letter to her in October of her junior year:

Dear Sam,

I am writing this letter because lately, we have been fighting a lot about school, and I want to explain some things to you without us screaming at each other. I hope that I can communicate my feelings better to you in writing.

I want you to know that the only reason Dad and I have been involved in your schooling is because we love you and want to help, not, as you have suggested, to punish you. When you were diagnosed with ADHD many years ago, the school offered to give you extra help with 504 accommodations. At the time, and over the years, we were so pleased because many of the things provided were helpful to you. But I can see now that you are having a hard time with the extra attention and help being offered, so that is what I want to discuss with you.

504 accommodations are not required for you to remain in high school. They are there to help you, not to embarrass you. It's something that kids with ADHD and other learning issues are lucky to have available to them so they won't get lost in the public school system. As you well know, most teachers are not very accommodating to kids who don't fit the mold of a "typical" student. With a 504 available to you, you have a better chance to be successful in high school and go on to college well-prepared. We have seen so much improvement from you over the years, but college being only two years away is why we are paying so much more attention and trying to help you now more than ever.

Obviously, the ultimate goal is for you to learn to schedule your time, do your homework, and study for tests without extra help from your teachers, Dad, or me. As you recently said, you are the one who has to motivate yourself to want to do the work and do the best you can for yourself. I know you are trying to work on this because I have seen you become so much more independent since you began high school. I also know you are trying much harder this year to improve your grades, and I am so proud of you for that. Sometimes, though, it doesn't appear to Dad or me that you are doing the best you can in some areas because we see so much else going on in your life. A progress report in English and a call from your history teacher reinforce our suspicions. I guess the reason we are so concerned is that this is such an important year for making college decisions that will be based on your academic performance. I know this can be an overwhelming thought, but we are here to help you through this.

I understand that you are older and feel uncomfortable about getting extra attention because of your ADHD and believe that you don't need the help. This is totally *understandable, and I will support your effort to be more independent. Something you have to decide, then, is whether you are ready to make schoolwork a priority over your social life, computer, phone, and TV so you won't need the extra help. I know that just getting through the day at school is an effort for you sometimes, but you have to keep in mind that you don't have many other responsibilities in your life besides going to school and doing your homework. We don't ask much of you around the house or that you get a job to earn spending money. So, I want you to think about putting more time into your schoolwork now so you won't look back later on and regret not having done more.*

Something else I've been thinking about is that you said I treat you differently than Dana, as if that is a bad thing. I hope that you would want me to treat the two of you differently since you have two very different personalities. You know that I love you both with all my heart and for who you each are, not because you are the same. I respond to each of you in different ways, as I think I should. As you know, one of my favorite things to do with you is cuddle on the couch, watch TV together, and talk about whatever is on your mind at the time. Dana shies away from things like that, and that's okay, but I would never stop doing that with you just because Dana doesn't like it, nor would I expect Dana to do something with me that makes her feel uncomfortable just because you like it. So, what I'm getting at with schoolwork is that you have different needs than Dana. Just because Dana didn't require extra help and did her homework late at night doesn't mean that you shouldn't get extra help when needed or that working late at night is right for you.

We don't expect you to get all As. We expect you to do the best you can. I know it's hard to follow in Dana's footsteps, but

I don't think you give yourself enough credit. You are a smart, beautiful, and loving person who happens to have ADHD, which is nothing to be ashamed of. You have a physical problem that causes you to lose attention and concentration easily. As responsible parents, Dad and I got you the proper medication and help we felt you needed in school. If you had diabetes, you would be on insulin and might have special provisions with the nurse each day to check your blood levels or tutors available when you didn't feel well enough to be in school. Not much different, if you ask me!

So, my little Sammy, let's stop fighting about school and see if we can find a middle ground to move forward. You know I love you and only want you to be happy.

I love you forever,
Mom

When I wrote that letter to Sam, I wasn't quite sure what the outcome would be. I hoped at least some of what I'd written would get through to her.

Not too long after Sam read my letter, she agreed to have a tutor in chemistry—a class for which she'd gotten a D in the first marking period. With the extra help, she raised that grade to a C+ the next marking period and, much to my amazement, an A in the last two. In hindsight, Sam and I both agreed that the one-on-one attention from a special tutor, who respected Sam's limitations and found ways to help her retain the information, was priceless. But, even without tutors in her other subjects, Sam managed to raise all of her C grades, except one, to As and Bs in each of the last two marking periods that year.

I'm pretty sure that Dana's being away at college during that year contributed to Sam's change in attitude and heightened interest in her academic success. Being the only child at home and becoming the center of our attention—in a positive way this time—appeared to help Sam come out of hiding from what she perceived to be the constant attention we showered on Dana before she left for college.

When Sam decided—on her own without my prodding—to start an SAT review course to help improve her scores, I knew something had clicked. I felt like I'd made a positive impact with my letter. For the first time, I began to believe that college—which had seemed unlikely for Sam at many points over the years—was a possibility for our younger daughter after all.

When I picked Sam up from school to get her hair and nails done for prom, I could tell something was up. In our town, prom was a big deal, so when a senior had invited Sam a month or two earlier, she'd gladly accepted. Leading up to the event, she'd bought a new dress, booked hair and nail appointments, and spent hours on the phone making plans with her friends. Today, however, felt off. I knew she was excited about going to prom, but I sensed she was nervous as well.

She was pretty quiet at the two appointments and on our way home. And when she saw my mother-in-law sitting in her car in our driveway as we drove up to our house, her face fell.

Oh no. I'd forgotten to tell her that her Grandma Carol was coming over to see her dress and partake in the pre-prom festivities.

If looks could kill! Glaring at me, Sam yelled, "Why is Gramma here? You know how I feel about the way she treats me! I don't want her to come upstairs or to be here while I'm getting ready. You have to tell her to go home!" With that, she jumped out of the car, ran into the house without saying hello to her grandmother, and went up to her room.

Trying to hide my uneasiness, I walked inside with Carol and asked her to wait in the living room while I checked on Sam. By the time I got upstairs, Sam was crying in the bathroom. In between sobs, she blurted out, "I hate my hair and the makeup too!"

I could tell she didn't want my input, so I stood by quietly, waiting for her next move. She wiped off her makeup and pulled down her hair, then began to redo both to her liking. By the time she was done, she was calmer and let me help her into her dress.

I breathed a sigh of relief, knowing that her ride was due in ten minutes and she was almost out the door. But before I could suggest that she go down to show her grandmother, Sam started crying again.

"I hate my dress!" she shouted. "I can't wear it. I'm going to see if there's something better in Dana's closet."

At this point, I ran downstairs, apologized to Carol—who had heard most of what was happening—and asked her to please leave. I felt bad about it, but given their history, I knew that having her there during Sam's meltdown was a mistake.

By the time I ran back upstairs and reached Sam, she had already taken off her dress and was trying on one of Dana's from a prior prom. Of course, it didn't fit—they were totally different sizes—so she put hers back on just as her ride arrived.

After a quick parting wave, "Hurricane Sam" ran out of the house, leaving a trail of destruction in her wake. I was an emotional wreck, Carol was upset and insulted, and I was left to clean up the mess in the bathroom and in Dana's and her bedrooms.

When I finally pulled myself—and the house—together, I sat down to reflect on what had just happened. It felt like a blast from the past when Sam had little control of her emotions. It reminded me of that terrible Thanksgiving Day many years earlier when she had ripped her clothes off in the middle of the living room and I'd had to carry her into the bathroom to calm her down.

But this doesn't diminish the huge progress she's made this year, I reminded myself. The thought made me feel a little better. I knew that Sam would continue to have days like this throughout her life, but I relied on her positive progress to feed my hope for her continued growth and maturity. And I promised myself that I would always support her through difficult times like this one, no matter what.

10

SO CLOSE, YET SO FAR

WITH JUST ONE MORE YEAR of high school to go, I hoped for Sam's positive momentum from the prior year to continue in twelfth grade—and when I saw the report card for her first marking period, my hopes were rewarded. I smiled with pride as I learned that Sam had made the honor roll for the very first time! Unfortunately, the drama that ensued shortly afterward overshadowed this academic success.

A few months into the first semester, Sam's science teacher, Mrs. O'Brien, left me a disturbing voicemail: "Hi, Mrs. Kaufman, this is Sam's science teacher. Recently, Sam has been calling out excessively, and her going to the bathroom is becoming an issue. But, when I confronted Sam about these issues, she was disrespectful and confrontational."

This was a teacher who had been hyper-critical of Sam and had belittled the symptoms of her disability since the beginning of the school year, so I was taking all of this in with a grain of salt.

"Although I know Sam has ADHD," Mrs. O'Brien continued, "I expect her to be more respectful and less confrontational, and she must follow the rules regarding the bathroom. Otherwise, I will have to take away her privileges." She ended by saying, "I believe that Sam's behavior is unacceptable, regardless of her ADHD."

After receiving this troublesome message, I immediately called Sam's guidance counselor to request that Mrs. O'Brien be at our next 504 meeting, which was scheduled for December. Maybe I'd get through to her better if I had the administration present to back me up.

"I am having a big problem with Sam's lack of attention, fidgeting with things on her desk, asking to use the bathroom, and calling out during class," Mrs. O'Brien launched right in when we started the meeting in December. "I have tried, but nothing is working to help Sam change these behaviors."

The assistant principal jumped in first. "You do realize that much of the problems you are describing are typical ADHD issues, right? If you take another look at her 504 Plan, you will see suggestions to help you guide Sam into reducing some of these problems in your classroom. I think it would be beneficial if we set up a meeting with me, you, and Sam to strategize ways to help defuse the situation."

Much to all of our dismay, Mrs. O'Brien just shook her head and held her ground. "That's not necessary," she said firmly. "I'll take care of this by myself."

Sure, you will, I thought with an inward groan. I tried to press the issue, but Mrs. O'Brien wouldn't budge. I had a feeling that things were not going to get any better with this particular teacher anytime soon—if ever.

As I feared, Mrs. O'Brien continued to criticize and belittle Sam in the months that followed—which in turn resulted in our daughter becoming more confrontational. From Sam's feedback, we sensed that the situation had escalated out of control.

One afternoon after school—on a day Sam was home sick—a friend of hers called with an interesting story. "Sam, you're not going to believe this," she said. "Someone was talking during class today, and Mrs. O'Brien yelled, 'Sam, you need to stop talking and sit down now!' So, I said to her, 'Um, Sam isn't here. She's home sick today.' Crazy, right?"

Crazy indeed. Not sure how to handle this, we tried to get Sam to be more attentive in class and to try to avoid situations that would annoy her teacher. But things continued to deteriorate, and the situation came to a head in March when we received a troubling email:

> dear mr and mrs kaufman
>   just to inform you that sam and another student lost ten pts from their test due to talking while the test was still in progress
>   entire class was warned before test—not to mention previous tests
>   she argues after the fact
>   she is fortunate it is only ten points
>   sincerely Mrs O'Brien

The anger and frustration contained in that email were obvious, given the tone and lack of punctuation. That same week, she moved Sam's seat to the back of the classroom, disregarding the 504 Plan requirement that she be seated in front near the teacher. Sam said that when Mrs. O'Brien did this, she told her, "I'm moving you to the back of the room because I don't want to look at you anymore."

Shortly after this incident, Sam tried to talk to her teacher about finding an agreeable time to use the bathroom without disturbing the class since that was one of her biggest complaints. Mrs. O'Brien refused to discuss the situation with Sam, so Sam went to the assistant principal for advice. The assistant principal knew what was going on with the two of them, so she set up a meeting with Sam, the teacher, and herself for the next day.

Prior to that meeting, Mrs. O'Brien sent me another disturbing and angry email. Unfortunately, I didn't see it until after her meeting with Sam and the assistant principal.

> *. . . sam goes to the bathroom each day*
>
> *she is relentless in her outbursts and persistant determination to get her desires:*
>
> *she has a very negative effect on the class and instruction and creates much unnecessary chaos we were told to limit bathroom for student safely*
>
> *iit is in her best interest to be in class for all reasons*
>
> *if you would like to grant permissiion for sam to continue going to the bathroom regularly..*
>
> *i ask that you write a note accepting full responsibility for her safety and full responsiblily for missed work*
>
> *she needs me to reexplain material upon her arrival, or she corresponds with another student to catch up, but in doing so, both sam and the other person fall behind*
>
> *my goal is to keep her focused so her grades are good, however, i am having great difficulty*
>
> *moving her seat results in confrontatiion*
>
> *removing her bag with lotion, phone, lipstick, headbands, etc does too*
>
> *perhaps it would be in sam's best interest to leave these items in her car, since she is easily distracted*
>
> *she removed her hairband during a lab involving fire. i spoke with her,*
>
> *but she knew the requirements and still "pushed"....safety is grounds for lab removal and a zero....but in lite of her circumstances i try to work with her.*
>
> *i have even put her with a lab group that results in her success*

funny thing is, she doesnt seem to work with me at all....
i also alliowed her to make up a detention for class dis-
ruption last friday.
..again accommodating her as much as possible
i certainly hope she shows up today for the detention
sincerely,
Mrs O'Brien

In the fourteen years that our children had attended school in that district, we had never received a more unprofessional, immature, or inappropriate correspondence from a teacher. Had I read this email before they met, I would have insisted on being present at the meeting—but I didn't see it until it was too late.

I was later informed that Mrs. O'Brien asked to speak first, refused to look at Sam, and verbally attacked her during the course of the meeting, even calling her a liar. Sam was too upset to communicate what she had originally wanted to say and left the meeting in tears.

Given everything that had transpired, I decided to reach out to the superintendent of schools to see if she could help defuse the situation. It saddened me to have taken this action with only two months left in Sam's senior year, but given the circumstances, we felt it would be an injustice to Sam if we did not bring this unfortunate situation to the attention of someone in a position of power in the district.

"Given the provision in Sam's 504 Plan that indicates her teachers must develop cues to assist Samantha to identify off-task and inattentive behaviors and to refocus her on tasks and presentations, I'm confused at why things have escalated to this level," Sam's principal began.

After receiving my request, the superintendent met with the principal, who in turn organized a meeting for the following week with himself, the teacher, the assistant principal, Sam's guidance counselor, an Education Association representative for the teacher, Barry, and me—and now here we all were. The atmosphere in the room was tense, to say the least, and everyone seemed to be on edge. I was relieved that I had come prepared with a list of concerns, questions, and expectations. Given the nature of our complaints and the combative attitude Mrs. O'Brien had displayed in the past, I was extremely nervous.

"Since it appears that you haven't implemented any cues for Sam to focus on," the principal continued, "I want you to meet with the district's Learning Disabilities Teacher Consultant, who will assist you in addressing strategies to help."

Mrs. O'Brien made no immediate response, so I went next—beginning with addressing her voice messages and emails.

"Can you please explain to us what your intention was in leaving me such an unprofessional voicemail and why you believe Sam's behavior is unacceptable regardless of ADHD?" I demanded. "It is as if you refuse to accept the fact that Sam has a disability. Then, there were the two angry emails you sent and the fact that when Sam displays behaviors typical of children with ADHD, you address them with her in front of the entire class rather than talking to her privately. As Sam's parents, we have lost confidence in you as an educator after the way you have disregarded Sam's 504 Plan and the input we've given you about Sam feeling threatened when someone tries to control her in a negative way. We've explained to you more than once that her lack of self-control causes her to retaliate in what appears to be a disrespectful manner. So, I guess I want to know since you've refused to meet with the assistant principal for help and input on how to fix the problems you are having, what specifically have you done to try and help Sam on your own?"

Mrs. O'Brien cleared her throat and said, "Mrs. Kaufman, I want you to know that it was never my intention to be negative. Rather, I was trying to be informational. It appears I was given mixed messages from the beginning. I wish you had called me more often—and obviously, I wish we could have handled this matter privately. Unfortunately, there has been 'miscommunication' on how to handle taking points off tests and giving Sam detention for her perceived behavior problems in class. I was also concerned about safety issues during labs and when Sam was going to the bathroom."

After listening to the teacher's attempt at explaining herself, the principal jumped back in. "Although you indicated that your email correspondences and telephone message were intended to be informational, that's not how they were perceived by Mrs. Kaufman or those of us who read the emails and listened to the voicemail," he said. "Clearly, they would have been communicated in a far better and clearer manner if you'd spoken directly to Sam's mom on the phone or in a parent conference. This would have allowed you to discuss detailed information related to Sam's classroom decorum and academic performance in a more professional manner. Going forward, try to avoid future interactions that may be interpreted by Sam as ridiculing or getting personal in front of the class. I expect you to be positive, firm, and fair."

At that point, the guidance counselor spoke up with, "I have a suggestion. I am going to find someone from the Child Study Team to work with you to help find solutions to defuse the situation and eliminate the apparent power struggle you are having with Sam."

Mrs. O'Brien didn't look particularly pleased with any of this, but she didn't have much choice but to go along with the guidance counselor's recommendation. We ended the meeting with a new path forward.

I was pleased that school officials had gone to bat for us and been diligent in addressing our concerns in a professional manner at that meeting. But what pleased me the most were the intangible benefits that resulted.

An administrator in the school district who was not present at our meeting but was aware of what was going on with Sam asked if I would meet with her the following week.

After some initial small talk, she got to the point. "I heard about your meeting with Sam's teacher and some of the administrators at the high school," she said. "I want you to know there is a concern in the district that a majority of our staff have an inadequate understanding of learning disabilities, particularly of ADHD. Many teachers inappropriately have the same standards for all students in their classrooms and are not ready to accept the responsibility of deviating from their strict set of rules and expectations. I want to assure you that no matter what happens with Sam's teacher going forward, you have raised everyone's level of consciousness about ADHD and that, given the nature of your concerns, I have highlighted the need for our district to take a closer look at issues relating to ADHD in the classroom, especially at the high school level."

I was smiling as I left her office that day. After twelve years of struggling through the school system with Sam, I felt a sense of satisfaction knowing that my unwavering determination in advocating for my daughter may have finally paid off. I wished for Sam's sake that it could have happened sooner, but at least other kids with ADHD in our school district would have a better chance at being understood going forward.

I arrived home from work one day in April of Sam's senior year, and after collecting the day's mail from our box, I noticed an envelope from one of the colleges Sam had applied to. I couldn't wait to get inside—I had to know—so I ripped the envelope open right where I stood, and there it was: Sam's first acceptance!

I ran into the house and, unable to contain my excitement, called Barry at work. "Barr, she did it! Sam got her first acceptance letter! She's going to college!"

I could hear the smile in his voice when he said, "Well, what do you know! That's terrific. We'll have to celebrate tonight."

Sam's successful journey through the college application process was a testament to her own perseverance and ability to succeed, especially given how disruptive the situation with Mrs. O'Brien had been that year. She viewed her SAT review course as a vehicle to the next stage in her life and had put in the extra effort to improve her grades. We'd also hired a college counselor to help her navigate the admissions process, hoping to eliminate the power struggle that typically ensued when Barry or I intervened with her schoolwork. And it had worked!

Pride blossomed in my chest as I stared down at the letter in my hand. Given the ups and downs of her primary school experiences and the difficulties ADHD had created in her life, I had often doubted whether Sam would be able to attend college. But she'd put in the work, and her SAT scores and GPA had proven high enough to earn her a spot at a good school—and not just one. As it turned out, in the weeks to come, a few more acceptance letters would arrive.

The tears in my eyes at that moment were brought on by a myriad of emotions. Although I had no idea what was yet to come for Sam in the years to follow, I celebrated her accomplishment with excitement and deep gratification. I hadn't given up on my daughter, and her ultimate success was the best vindication of my continued advocacy on her behalf that I could have hoped for.

As I think about the innumerable confrontations Sam had with her teachers and the conflicts I encountered while advocating for my daughter throughout her school years, one question always forces itself to the front of my mind: *Were my expectations of Sam's teachers too high?*

At times, I wondered if Sam should have been placed in a special education class where she would have received individualized attention. However, after having her tested and meeting with a team of school administrators, guidance counselors, and teachers, it was clear to everyone that she did not meet the standards for a special ed program. With this option off the table, our only alternative for keeping her in the public school system was to arrange for 504 accommodations and keep her in a regular classroom.

I understand that the overt symptoms of ADHD often placed a tremendous burden on both Sam and her teachers. Self-control, organization, and sitting at a desk for hours seemed to be an impossible task for my daughter at times, and I, more than anyone, can empathize with how difficult dealing with Sam's outbursts, constant fidgeting, missed assignments, and disruptive behavior must have been for many of her teachers. But even taking all this into consideration, I do not believe that my expectations were unreasonable or unattainable. In fact, to take it one step further, I believe that my high standards were 100 percent necessary and should be met by all teachers who touch the lives of students with disabilities.

Everything I have read about ADHD over the last two decades states one thing in particular with conviction: ADHD is a neurobiological disability. I firmly believe that children with ADHD do not "choose" to act the way they do and that many of their actions are overt symptoms of a disability. Unfortunately, many of Sam's teachers did not view her conduct from the same perspective. Sam's behavior often came across to these teachers as disrespectful, lazy, or dishonest. When her needs were perpetually minimized or outright ignored by these educators despite our frequent reminders that she needed extra consideration, when she was given detention for calling out in class, when she had points taken off for missing homework assignments (later found in the bottom of her knapsack), or when she was called a liar by an angry teacher, it became clear to me that convincing them otherwise was a losing battle.

I learned many years after Sam graduated from high school that the negative reactions and hurtful tactics used against her were not unique to teachers in our district or that period of time. Not too long ago, in fact, I heard a disturbing story from the mother of a boy with ADHD about him being asked to stand in front of the classroom while his teacher went to sit at his desk, where she started imitating his behavior by calling out, talking to the other students, and fidgeting with things around her. After doing all of this, the teacher looked up at the boy and asked, "Do you think you could teach a lesson with this type of disruptive behavior going on?" How humiliating!

I was horrified when I heard this story—which, to me, spotlighted the lack of respect some teachers continue to have for students with ADHD. Although I recognize that there is additional training available for educators today, I have learned from experience that the training teachers receive is only as good as their ability to implement what they have learned in an effective and humane manner. Based on the story above, it appears that some teachers are still struggling to find a successful way to handle disruptions in their classrooms. I think we can all agree that humiliating or embarrassing a child in front of their peers, punishing a child for actions out of their control, or calling a child names is unacceptable conduct for a teacher and should fall short of any parent's expectations.

Years after Sam finished high school, I opened the file where I kept all of her old school records and reviewed her report cards. I expected to find poor grades in the courses with the teachers who complained about her the most. Instead, I found the opposite to be true. Somehow, Sam managed to earn As and Bs as her final year-end grades in all of those classes. It's taken me a while to figure out how to interpret this outcome, which went against every frustrated educator's assumption that Sam's behavior was getting in the way of her academic success. After turning it over and over in my mind, I've come to believe that those teachers were so focused on Sam's behavior in class that they blinded themselves to how well she was doing on assignments and tests. Had they been less combative and more willing to take a different approach with Sam, I believe they would have seen a positive change in her attitude and behavior and appreciated her for the smart girl she was.

It's not unreasonable to expect that students with disabilities be treated with respect and sensitivity. Parents should not have to work as hard as I did to open the eyes of unprepared, unsympathetic teachers—teachers who would rather battle with a student and try to mold them into something they're not rather than meet them halfway. It's appalling to me that so many of Sam's teachers seemed to believe that only one type of student should be in a classroom: a student without disabilities.

I am so proud of Sam for overcoming the obstacles her teachers threw in her path over the years, for her ability to rise above their insensitivity and lack of understanding, and for how she ultimately succeeded on her own terms.

At the end of Sam's senior year, as I sat in the high school gymnasium waiting for the graduation procession to begin, I found myself reflecting on the previous eighteen years and what had transpired to help Sam reach this milestone moment.

You did it, Sammy! I thought, my heart filled with pride and joy as I watched her walking toward me in her cap and gown with her friends by her side. I felt the struggles and uncertainties of the past slowly melt away, replaced by an overwhelming sense of accomplishment and triumph at Sam's ability to reach this monumental event in her life—and my ability to survive the turmoil that preceded it.

A snapshot of that moment will remain in my mind and in my heart forever.

With my optimism in high gear and high school in the rearview mirror, I looked toward the future and what was yet to come for my Sam as she prepared to head off for college in a few months.

11

THE CONTRACT

I EXPECTED THE SUMMER BEFORE SAM left for college to be filled with the excitement of finding out who her roommate would be, shopping for dorm room necessities, choosing her classes, and other typical preparations for going off to school.

Then, her boyfriend broke up with her.

I understand that many teenage girls suffer deeply when their first love breaks up with them. But when Sam was blindsided by her boyfriend's decision to end their relationship a few weeks before her departure for college, her reaction made all of her previous meltdowns and emotional outbursts pale in comparison.

Barry and I were in the kitchen when we heard Sam crying in her room.

Her best friend, Jenna, was in there with her. I heard her trying to calm her down. "Sam, it's going to be okay," she reassured her. "It's probably better that you go to college without a long-distance boyfriend anyway."

Not hearing a response from Sam, I started to head to her room to see if I could help. Before I even reached the stairs, she came running out of her room, sobbing uncontrollably.

"I can't believe he just did that to me!" she cried. "We were going to a party tonight, but he just broke up with me instead."

Realizing that when Sam was in this state, there was nothing I could do to reach her. I stood back and watched her stumble down the stairs and out of the house, breaking the screen door in the process. Jenna trailed after her with a worried look on her face.

Barry and I were, understandably, concerned by what we had just witnessed—and what might happen next. If Jenna hadn't been with Sam, we likely would have gone after her. Instead, I yelled after them, "PLEASE call me with an update, Jen. I need to know that she's okay."

She nodded and waved a distracted goodbye as she hurried to catch up with our distraught daughter.

It seemed like an eternity before the phone rang. "Aim, we're up the street at her now ex-boyfriend's house," Jenna reported. "I'm really worried, though. Sam just threw herself onto the driveway, and she's crying and screaming for him to come out. I have never seen her act this way." She sounded afraid—not for herself, but for Sam.

"Can you try to bring her home?" I asked. She kept me on the line as she tried desperately to calm Sam down and persuade her to get up off of the ground, but nothing worked. I debated whether or not Barry and I should go get her, but I didn't want to make a bad situation worse. The alarm in Jenna's voice made me realize that this was not a typical reaction to a high school breakup. Sam's emotional stability, and possibly her safety, was at risk here.

"I'm going to hang up and let you continue trying," I said after some quick deliberating, "but call me if things get worse. And I will call you back as soon as I can figure out what to do next. Thank you so much for staying there with her."

When I hung up the phone, I was unnerved. Envisioning Sam lying on another family's driveway in such a vulnerable state was disturbing.

I knew Barry and I couldn't handle this alone, so I picked up the phone and dialed Sam's pediatrician. When I was done explaining the situation to Dr. Cohen, she paused for a moment. Then she made a suggestion I didn't expect.

"I think you should call her friend and tell her that if Sam doesn't get up and come home in the next five minutes, you will call the police," she said decisively. "And make sure she understands that if you do that, they will bring her to the hospital for evaluation. But keep in mind that once you put this plan into action, you have to be ready to follow through."

"Are you sure?" I asked, my heart breaking for my already heart-broken daughter.

"Do you have any other ideas?" she asked me.

I searched my heart and soul before making that call to Sam's friend—and after I did, even though I am not very religious, I prayed that Sam would walk through the door before the five-minute time limit ran out so I wouldn't have to be making a second call, this time to the police.

Although I knew that sending Sam to the hospital might be the most responsible thing for me to do, I agonized over my decision.

Thankfully, Sam came stumbling into the house a few minutes later. Overcome with relief, I immediately turned my attention to helping her through this crisis, one hug at a time. Neither of us talked about what had just happened right away. I just followed her into her room, climbed into bed with her, and held her in my arms, hopeful that giving her comfort and love would begin the healing process and help lessen the hurt and anger that had triggered her emotional meltdown.

I look back on that night with a conflicted heart. Some might think that threatening to call the police on your own child—and meaning it—is a terrible thing for a mother to do. But most of those people haven't raised a child with ADHD or another disability that limits impulse control. Sam reacted far more intensely to typical high school drama than the average teenager, so I often found it necessary to evaluate situations in a different light than the average parent probably would. If I had to do it all over again with the benefit of hindsight, I believe that I would make the same decision. My job was to protect my troubled daughter from hurting herself and to get her the help she needed, and that's what I did that day.

What might have happened next if Sam had not walked back in through the broken screen door that night is something I try not to focus on. Instead, I remind myself of the inner strength Sam displayed as she battled through the pain and took control by picking herself up from the driveway and getting herself home in time. I also focus on how following my maternal instincts once again proved to be the right—the only—course of action to help my daughter.

I assume that bringing a child to college for the first time is a day of mixed emotions for most parents. When we dropped Dana at school, I was excited and apprehensive at the same time. I was so proud of her accomplishments, yet I worried about the typical things that concern parents at that stage in their child's life. Would she get along with her roommate? Would she make friends easily? Would the work be too hard?

When it was time to bring Sam to college two years later, I experienced all of those emotions again, but on top of that, I also had major concerns about how she would manage her ADHD now that she would be on her own. In preparation for this transition, we arranged for Sam to receive accommodations from the Department of Disability Services, and I scheduled an appointment for her to meet with the director of the department before we left campus.

On the first day, we met Sam's roommates, unpacked her stuff, and organized a dinner with some of the girls and their families. Our appointment wasn't until 1 p.m. the following day, so we took Sam to buy her books and help her acclimate to her new surroundings in the morning. For the moment—and I stress the word *moment*—it appeared that Sam was handling this major transition in her life rather well. I was cautiously optimistic that everything was going to be just fine, and she would be ready to stand on her own two feet when we left her later that afternoon.

My good feelings quickly faded, however, when we approached the front door of the Department of Disability Services a few minutes before our appointed time and Sam refused to enter.

"Come on, Sammy," I coaxed her. "It won't take long! I just want you two to meet each other so you have a resource to lean on if you need it."

"Just a few minutes and we'll be out of here," Barry tried next.

Sam sat down on a bench and started to cry. "I won't go in," she insisted. "I don't need special disability services or medication! I'll be fine. Trust me, I can do this."

I tried to stay calm, but anger and frustration got the best of me. Trying not to create a scene and hoping my voice could not be heard across campus, I said through gritted teeth, "Look, Sam, we talked about this over the summer. You agreed you would continue to take medication at college and would utilize the special resources available to students with ADHD. What changed all of a sudden?"

"I won't go in," she sobbed, rocking in her seat. "I don't want to be different!"

My anger quickly evaporated. Sam was embarrassed—worried that she would be the only one of her new friends in need of medication and extra help. I couldn't blame her. After all, who would want to be set apart like that right at the beginning of college, a place that was supposed to be a fresh start?

We tried to talk her into the meeting for a bit longer, but eventually, we realized that there was no way to persuade her to set foot inside that building. The only thing we could do was acquiesce, cut the strings, and hope she would figure it out on her own.

Once Sam felt confident that we weren't going to force the issue, she calmed herself down and convinced us that it was okay to leave.

Saying goodbye to my daughter after seeing her in so much turmoil just moments before was gut-wrenching. I'm not quite sure how I got myself into the car, but as soon as we pulled away, my emotions took over, and I began to cry. I blamed myself for not doing a better job preparing Sam for this transition. *Where did I go wrong?* I wondered. *What could I have done differently? Would she have reacted differently if the department was called Special Services instead of "Disability" Services?* There was no way of knowing—and at this point, I knew it wouldn't make a difference anyway. Trying to stay positive, I hoped that she would find her way and figure out how to succeed at college in spite of her shaky beginning. But deep inside, I had a feeling that things might get much worse before they got better.

"Hi, Mom, I have good news," Sam announced at the beginning of a call home in her first few weeks at school. "My friends and I are going to rush a sorority next month. I'm so excited. It's going to be so much fun!"

I was surprised—and a little dismayed—that students at her college were allowed to do this so soon, and I voiced my apprehension to Sam. "Look, baby girl, knowing how social you are, I'm concerned that you will fall behind in your classes if you're focused on rushing a sorority. Since you aren't taking your medication or getting extra help, how do you plan on keeping up with the work?"

"Oh, Mom, don't worry," she said in a tone that made clear she was barely listening. "I will be able to do both. Really, don't worry!"

Yeah, right! How many times had I heard that before?

In the months that followed, we heard a lot about rushing sororities but little about Sam's classes, which we soon found out had fallen all the way to the bottom of her priority list. Missing morning classes and failing to hand in assignments became the norm for our daughter.

When Sam arrived home for winter break, it was with the news that she had a 1.9 GPA and had earned only nine credits for the entire semester—a performance that meant she was officially on academic probation. Barry and I weren't particularly surprised—but we weren't happy, either. We decided it was time to take charge of this unfortunate situation, so we sat her down for a talk.

"Don't be so concerned about my grades," Sam began right away, trying to sugarcoat the situation. "After all, my college allows a student to fall below a 2.0 and be on academic probation for three semesters before expelling them from school. I'll do better next semester—I promise."

Of course, that wasn't going to work for us. Sam's school might allow three semesters of such low performance, but one semester was *our* limit.

"We don't care what the stipulations at your school are," Barry said. "Since we are paying for your tuition, we expected much more from you. Earning only nine credits in your first semester is unacceptable. Deep down, we know this is the perfect college for you, and we believe that you are capable of doing the work if you put your mind to it."

I took over from there. "So, here's what we are willing to do. I wrote up a contract that we are all going to sign. Here are the things we expect from you if you want to stay in college for the spring semester and the following year and if you want us to pay your sorority dues: Schedule and attend appointments with your doctor over winter break to determine which medication you should be taking. Meet with your academic advisor to set up a plan for receiving classroom accommodations. Arrange for tutors in classes you're struggling with. Attend all classes, hand in assignments, and attain a 2.0 or better for the spring semester. If you do this, we will continue to pay your tuition and sorority dues."

"I can't believe you don't trust me! And you're making me sign this!" Sam picked up the contract I'd just laid out before her and tossed it aside.

My body tensed. Was this the beginning of a tantrum?

Much to my surprise, she managed not to spiral—and, more importantly, she even took some responsibility. "I guess I did screw up the first semester by not doing some of the things you wanted me to do on day one. And I *really* want to be in the sorority . . . so, okay, I'll sign this." She retrieved the paper and signed it.

With the contract agreed upon and tucked away, we enjoyed the rest of winter break together, and two weeks later, we sent Sam back to school for her second semester—with all our fingers and toes firmly crossed.

We were happy to see that things started out on the right foot for the second semester. Sam arranged to receive class notes and tutors in courses that were giving her trouble, and she started taking her medication again. Hearing that she was attending classes and completing her assignments on time helped to bring back my cautious optimism. I was pleased to see that she was following through and taking the stipulations in the contract seriously.

As the weeks progressed, Sam began to focus more on her classes and gained confidence in her academic abilities, and, much to everyone's surprise—including her own—her grades began to improve. A big help in all of this was her realization that many of her friends also needed medication and academic assistance. When she stopped worrying about what others thought about her disability, it freed her up to get the help she needed to thrive.

When Sam's second-semester report card showed a 2.68 GPA, we were all ecstatic. It was clear to Barry and me that she was beginning to take college more seriously and was willing to put in the extra effort needed.

~

We were proud of Sam's new sense of accomplishment and hoped it would provide a solid foundation for her academic future. But we weren't ready to stop there. Since the contract had succeeded beyond our wildest expectations, why not keep that momentum going? With this thought in mind, we sat her down for another chat when she came home for summer break.

"We are so proud of you for pulling things together this semester," I began. "That contract we all signed back in December seems like it was the perfect tool for guiding you in the right direction. So, let's do another one for this upcoming fall semester. In addition to you doing everything you've been doing—taking your medication, seeking out classroom accommodations, attending all classes, and handing in assignments—we expect you to earn at least a 2.5 GPA. If you do, we will continue to pay your tuition and sorority dues, *and* we will pay for half of that spring break trip to Mexico you are planning."

"A 2.5?" she repeated. "That feels like a lot of pressure. Can't we change it to 2.3 or something lower than 2.5? *Please*? I know I did higher than that last semester, but some of the classes I'm planning to take this semester seem like they will be much harder."

"Look, Sam, I don't feel that our expectations are unrealistic," Barry jumped in. "I honestly believe that you can do this—so much so that I'm willing to risk losing the deposit we put down on your trip already in order to stick to this new agreement. Go back to school with a positive attitude, and let's see what happens."

After Sam returned to college in the fall, she sometimes called me crying and saying, "Mom, please, the pressure is too much. My friends can't believe that you won't let me go to Mexico if I don't get a 2.5. Can't you guys be more flexible?"

I was tempted to give in, but Barry made me stand my ground. He took the phone from me and told a crying Sam, "If your friends don't believe us, then put them on the phone so they can hear it directly from me. You need to get a 2.5, or you're not going to Mexico. I know you can do this, Sam—so have faith in yourself and believe you can do it also!"

I was speechless when Sam's grades were posted a few months later and she had a 2.92 GPA. Clearly, our contracts had helped redirect her priorities toward reaching the goals we had set for her—and more! Her improvement in school did not go unnoticed by her professors, either. She began to receive positive feedback from them as her grades climbed. Although there were some bumps in the road along the way, Sam continued to maintain an above-average GPA and successfully navigated her way through the next two semesters.

In the past, when Barry and I disagreed about Sam's issues, he had typically deferred to my point of view. For many years, this had made sense since he didn't have a great track record when it came to dealing with Sam. Throughout her childhood, his short temper, sarcasm, and defeated attitude had typically gotten in the way. But when he insisted that we not lower the GPA that she needed to go on spring break, I let him take the lead. In the end, his authoritative yet trusting approach with Sam was much more effective than the confrontational methods he'd used in the past.

Seeing this, I wondered how things might have turned out if I had let Barry lead the way more often. Would his harder-line approach have been effective in some situations? Or was it only working now because he'd learned to control his temper with Sam and remain positive even as he set firm boundaries? Regardless, it was clear that what he was doing now was working, and I began to seek his input more often when it came to Sam. Gratifyingly, I noticed that Sam's response to her father improved in return. It was reassuring to see my husband and younger daughter finding common ground after all these years—and to finally feel as though I had a true partner in my journey with Sam.

~

Since Sam only earned twenty-one credits her freshman year, we insisted that she take an online course that summer and find a paying internship that offered credits the following summer to make up for the deficit. She passed the online class without a problem, so I went online the spring semester of her sophomore year, researched her college's requirements for internships, and passed the information along to her.

On the morning of a required meeting, I called to make sure she was up and on the way.

After a few rings, I heard a sleepy-voiced Sam mumble, "Hellooo?"

"Sam, it's Mom," I said, my annoyance more than evident in my tone. "I'm calling to make sure you are up and ready to go to the meeting. But since you are obviously still in bed and it starts soon, I guess you won't be going. You do realize this was a required meeting for you to attend if you want to get credits for an internship, right? I can't believe you didn't set your alarm."

"Don't worry," she said hastily, "I'll make sure to get the information needed from the internship department. I'm sure that will be okay."

After hanging up, I sat there in a daze, wondering if Sam might have to go to summer school to make up the credits she was missing and agonizing over how much that would cost. I was still turning these thoughts over in my mind when my phone rang fifteen minutes later.

"O.M.G, Mom, wait until you hear this! It turns out that missing the meeting was the best thing that could have happened."

I couldn't imagine what Sam was about to say—the suspense was killing me!

Before I could press her for details, she said excitedly, "So, a few minutes after we hung up, I got a text from a friend who is working in New York City. She asked if I knew of anyone looking for a summer internship in the communications industry. She explained that someone they had previously hired changed their mind, leaving the position available. When she said it's a paid internship, and the person can earn credits, I told her that I was interested. Then I contacted the Internship Department to find out what I needed to do, and they gave me all the info I needed and said the position my friend told me about would totally qualify."

"That's amazing, Sam!" I said in a much brighter tone than I'd been able to muster earlier that morning. "Great job getting it all worked out."

After hanging up this time, I sat there smiling, thinking about the guardian angel I envisioned sitting on my daughter's shoulder and guiding her way.

12

CRAWLING TOWARD THE FINISH LINE

ALTHOUGH SAM'S GRADES AND ATTITUDE toward her studies had improved greatly since the first semester of her freshman year, Barry and I were hesitant when she broached the subject of studying in Barcelona during the second semester of her junior year. We were concerned about her living in a foreign country and wondered if her positive growth would continue without us being easily accessible. However, she had proven to us that she was more responsible for her actions and was using better judgment when making decisions, and we wanted to offer her a similar experience to Dana's studies abroad in London two years earlier.

After taking everything into consideration, and after Sam successfully argued her case and agreed to gather all of the information and make the arrangements necessary, we finally acquiesced. She and her roommate were responsible for finding the program and figuring out what travel documents and other necessities they needed, and if and when everything was accomplished on their end, Barry and I agreed we would book her flights for her.

When Sam arrived home for winter break and hadn't applied for her student visa yet, we saw our first red flag and considered canceling her flight. But when she found out that an agency in Boston could expedite the process, we kept our word and stuck to our original agreement. Luckily, her visa application did go through in time. So, with plans in place and travel documents in hand, we took her to the airport and walked her to the gate.

As we watched the "red tail lights heading to Spain," we crossed our fingers and hoped for the best.

My antennae immediately shot up when I heard Sam's soft, hesitant voice on the other end of the line. "So, Mom . . . what would you do if I came home with zero credits?"

I was speechless and couldn't believe what I was hearing. It took me a few minutes to process the implications of the bombshell she had just dropped. With a sick feeling in my stomach, I finally found the words to reply, "You're kidding, right?"

The first few months of the semester had seemed to go great. Sam enthusiastically shared her experiences of traveling to other countries and enjoying the hectic life in Barcelona while reassuring us that everything was going fine in her classes. It was only now, a few weeks before the end of the term, that I was finally getting the truth.

"Well, actually, I'm not kidding," she said, gaining steam. "So, here's what happened. My roommate and I decided we didn't need to attend most of our classes because we assumed we could catch up with the work by reading the books in time to pass our final exams. But today I realized I had fallen too far behind and might not be able to catch up, and I panicked. That's when I decided to call you."

My first thought was that I should bring her home immediately. But I wanted to give her a chance to rectify the situation—so, biting back the not-so-nice words I wanted to say, I kept my cool, controlled my voice, and said, "I'm really disappointed that you let things get this far. But what's done is done, so here's what you have to do: Go meet with your professors tomorrow morning. Arrange for tutors and ask if they will let you do extra work to raise your grades. Call me after so I know what they said—*before* I tell Daddy. He will go ballistic if you come home with no credits. Good luck. I'll talk to you tomorrow."

"Okay, Mom," she said meekly. "I'll try."

I kept my word and waited until I heard back from Sam the next day before telling Barry what was going on since I knew he would book her on the next flight home in the blink of an eye if I filled him in before she had something figured out. As soon as I found out that she had a plan in place, I broke the news to him. Needless to say, he was furious, but he ultimately agreed with me that we should let her stay and try to salvage the semester.

Sam spent the next few weeks studying and trying to make up the work. Without knowing her grades, she returned home for the summer to her disappointed parents with not much to say for herself.

Over the next couple of weeks, little by little, she confessed what the real problem had been. "I had trouble with a majority of my classes because of their concentration in Spanish," she admitted. "I guess not being able to be in the Liberal Arts program because I signed up too late was the problem. Too much Spanish."

"When I spoke to your program advisor before you left for Spain, she didn't feel that would be a problem," I said, unable to keep the edge out of my voice. "I guess that might have been true if you had attended your classes and applied a consistent effort throughout the semester. Unfortunately, that wasn't the case. But let's wait and see if you were able to lift your grades with your added efforts before we assume anything."

When Sam's grades arrived, we had a glimmer of false hope: She had raised her failing grade to a C-minus in two of her four classes, and we assumed that her last-minute studying had paid off. Then, we discovered that her college only accepted credits from other programs with grades of C or better. There was nothing we could do to convince the school in Spain to allow Sam to submit additional assignments or to convince her college in the US to accept a C-minus. So, she hadn't earned a single credit for the entire semester in Barcelona—and that meant she might not have enough credits to graduate the following spring.

As the summer progressed, Sam and I had many discussions about what had gone wrong in Spain. One day I asked her, "What did you think Dad and I would do when we found out that you skipped classes and were failing your courses?"

After a brief pause, she answered, "Actually, I didn't think."

Her honest admission struck a chord with me, reinforcing what I had read about kids with ADHD "living in the moment." They have difficulty learning from the past and rarely focus on how their actions will affect the future. Sam had repeated the same mistakes she made during her freshman year by putting her social life in Barcelona ahead of her studies. Lacking our hands-on input and ignoring our guidance from afar, she didn't consider the consequences until it was too late. Framed this way, I found it a lot easier to forgive her for not living up to our expectations.

Barry, on the other hand, was having a hard time moving past what he perceived as a serious breach of our trust on Sam's part. He didn't believe that ADHD was to blame for her poor behavior and lack of judgment while in Barcelona, and he was furious that she had lost an entire semester. To this day, in fact, he has a hard time hiding his disappointment about the money we wasted.

Needless to say, it was a tension-filled summer at the Kaufman household.

Even though Sam's semester abroad during her junior year fell short academically, something incredibly positive occurred in her personal life: Grandma Carol and a friend of hers traveled to Barcelona to visit Sam, and they actually had a good time together.

That's right—Sam and her grandma, who'd never seemed to get along, had spent time together and *enjoyed it*! Given their tumultuous history, I was shocked when I heard that Carol was booking a flight and making hotel reservations to visit Sam in Spain. But I kept my thoughts to myself and hoped for the best. I found out later that Carol had an ulterior motive for making that trip. Without telling anyone, she had decided it would be the perfect opportunity to try and mend her strained relationship with Sam. And it worked!

When Carol got back, she called to tell me what transpired. "I am so glad I went on this trip," she gushed. "The days I spent with Sam in Spain helped me view her in a new, more positive light. I finally realized that I couldn't change her, so I let go of the past and learned to love and accept her for who she is. We had lots of fun, and I believe we truly bonded in a different way that will help change our relationship going forward."

Boy was I surprised to hear this from Carol but so pleased with the outcome. And the call I received from Sam the next day validated what Carol had told me and so much more.

"Mom, it was great having Grandma Carol here!" she raved. "I was worried at first when I heard she was coming, but it was so much fun. We went sightseeing and ate at yummy restaurants. We got along great, and I definitely think our relationship will be so much better when I come home." Finally, Sam was feeling the love and affection from her grandmother whom she'd previously been convinced was reserved for her older sister. Much to everyone's delight, Carol's ulterior motive for the trip paid off big time.

As for me, I felt a new respect for Carol for finally accepting her role in the uncomfortable relationship she had with Sam and taking steps to rectify the situation. It warms my heart to see them together now and watch their love for each other continue to grow.

Witnessing my mother-in-law's acceptance of Sam helped ease some of the negative feelings I often had toward Carol and helped mend our tarnished relationship as well. During one of our heart-to-heart conversations about the early days, she reminded me that before Sam was diagnosed, she had given Barry an article about ADHD that was published in *Time Magazine*. She had sensed from early on that Sam had ADHD and hoped that the information might help guide us. At the time, I was angry at Carol for the way she treated Sam and me, and since the doctors and teachers we had consulted with all felt that Sam did not have ADHD, I rejected her input. In hindsight, I realize how detrimental my negative feelings toward Carol may have been—at the expense of my child's development. Had I been able to rise above my own feelings and let myself trust in Carol's special education training, things may have turned out differently. I will never know what difference an earlier diagnosis would have made for Sam, but I am glad that my relationship with my mother-in-law is better today than it ever has been before.

Given what happened in Barcelona, I thought about reinstituting Sam's contract before her senior year but ultimately decided against it. After all of our talks that summer, Sam understood that if she didn't pass all of her classes and earn two extra credits, she wouldn't be able to graduate with her friends. In this situation, graduation was the reward. Although I believe that what happened in Barcelona was mostly due to Sam's inability to foresee the consequences of her actions, I also believe that she needed to take responsibility for the outcome. All of us hoped for the best as Sam packed her car and headed back to college with a sense of determination and the will to succeed.

Halfway into Sam's first semester of her senior year, I decided to review her online transcript again to confirm exactly how many credits she needed to graduate—and I couldn't believe my eyes when I saw that the credit number for her semester abroad had been changed from zero to three earned credits.

Confused about how that happened, I called Sam's advisor to make sure it wasn't a big mistake. "Hi, this is Aimee Kaufman, Sam's mother. I wonder if you can explain to me how her semester in Barcelona went from zero credits when I looked in September to three credits two months later?"

"Hi, Mrs. Kaufman!" her advisor said cheerfully. "Yes, I'd be happy to explain. As a reminder, because Sam is classified with ADHD, her language requirement includes 'cultural courses' instead of traditional ones. So, Sam received three 'language elective' credits for studying in Barcelona in spite of her grades."

I was so relieved to find out that Sam had received credits just for being there! I already felt we'd made the right call allowing her to stay in Barcelona to complete the semester, and this new information confirmed that for me. If she'd left early, she wouldn't have earned those credits. Up until that point, I hadn't understood the importance of that one decision. After that phone call with her advisor, however, the enormity of the results came into focus with a jolt of complete surprise.

Throughout Sam's life, she had many up-and-down experiences with her medication. She went from Adderall to regular Ritalin to sustained release. When the effects started to wear off during school, we switched her to longer-lasting Concerta, which seemed to work better for a while. Then Sam wasn't eating well while on Concerta, so the doctor suggested that she try a non-stimulant medication called Strattera—but that wasn't as effective, so she went back on Concerta. Later, in college, Sam felt that wasn't working well, so she tried Adderall again, the first drug she had tried many years before—and that one was the winner.

Jumping from medication to medication like this was a frustrating roller coaster ride for Sam. I'm sorry to say that I didn't know to what extent until the last semester of her senior year in college.

After Sam was diagnosed with ADHD, I was quick to assume that most of her behavior problems were symptoms of the disability itself. But after reading a paper Sam wrote for one of her communication classes in college, I realized that many times I had been very wrong about my assumptions and had unintentionally overlooked—or perhaps misinterpreted—the symptoms listed on the insert I had stored away in the back of my mind.

I believe that my lack of knowledge regarding exactly what ADHD was while I was growing up made it hard for me to take control of it, which led my parents to put me on Adderall/ Ritalin (medication to help people with ADHD).

After being diagnosed, I think that everyone in my family will agree that ADHD became a scapegoat for most of our family disputes. Unable to defend my disability at the time, I had no choice but to accept the accusations that my behavior problems were the symptoms of ADHD. But ADHD medication has many side effects, including irritability and mood swings, and as it wears off, a feeling of slight depression can occur. As I became more educated about ADHD and the medication I was taking, I began to view my actions and interactions with my family in a different light. I believe that I often acted out due to the effects of my ADHD medication wearing off, something I was unable to understand or verbalize as a child. My parents' interpretation of my behavior, however, was that I was always acting out due to the fact that I have ADHD. To this day my parents typically interpret my rage and argumentative nature as the fact that I have ADHD.

I can vividly remember an instance in eighth grade that clearly illustrates this point. I had come home from school one day with a feeling of lethargy as my medication was wearing off. In my house, we were expected to do our homework after school—ironically, the same time of day that I became short-tempered and moody. At this stage in my life, I was starting to better understand my ADHD, making it easier for me to schedule my homework around the mood swings I endured while coming down from my medication. Unfortunately, my father wasn't aware of my new after-school schedule since he usually didn't get home from work until 8 p.m., and truthfully, I don't think he really wanted to understand, since he grew up in a very structured home and believed that homework must be completed before anything else.

When he arrived home earlier than usual on this particular afternoon, he asked me why I was watching television before my homework was done. The situation immediately escalated into a brawl between the two of us when I told him that I wanted to do my homework after dinner. As always, he attributed my disrespect for his expectations of me and my typical "bad" behavior to ADHD. We argued back and forth until he eventually gave up and walked away, stating that it was easier to just let me win. Although I got what I wanted, believe it or not, it always infuriated me when my father gave in to me without understanding my position.

Unable to find the right words, I silently placed the blame on my parents for putting me on a medication that made me feel such negative effects. I feel that my dad was so used to my high-tempered nature and blaming ADHD for all of my wrongdoings that he neglected to take into account that the medication had much to do with my response to him. This is something that has continued to anger me and has definitely put a strain on our family. But, as I think back to this argument, and many others I have had with my family members over the years, as frustrated as I was, I do recognize that I took no responsibility for the situations I helped create. It was easier for me to place the blame for my negative actions on my medication. I have come to realize, however, that although it's easier to blame the medication, I should try harder to control the side effects, even when it seems unbearable, so that one day my family and I can reach a common understanding.

Sam's poignant insights opened a window into the mind of a child suffering from the side effects of ADHD medication that someone who hasn't traveled down that road could only imagine. And, just as important, it opened the eyes and tugged at the heart of this unknowing mother. After reading Sam's paper, I wiped the tears from my eyes—and then read it again, and one more time after that. I felt ashamed for having missed the signs. Why hadn't I referred more often to that list of side effects?

After processing what Sam had written, I came to realize that I had expected the adverse reactions to the pills to occur while they were still in her body. Since I had never experienced the "crashing" effects of stimulant medication, and information about that kind of thing was not as readily available back then as it is now, it didn't occur to me that the symptoms referred to on that list might appear as the medication was wearing off or directly thereafter. As such, I always assumed that the negative behavior that followed was a symptom of Sam's ADHD. It never crossed my mind that it could be a direct effect of the medication itself.

Perhaps other parents might have figured out the correlation between the cycles of the drug and their child's up-and-down behavior. But I didn't—and after Sam pointed this out in her paper, I wondered why our doctors or the pharmaceutical company's insert didn't warn users of this apparently common occurrence. It saddens me to think that by the time I discovered this reality, it was too late to help Sam. I know I can never erase the innumerable after-school fights we had about homework and her lack of interest in school. But I am hoping that sharing what I've learned now will help other parents. If you are a parent of a child with ADHD, if you walk away with just one bit of new information after reading this book, I hope it is this extremely important fact about the "crashing" effects of many ADHD medications. I learned it too late to help Sam, but maybe it's not too late to help your children.

Sam's paper not only opened my eyes to the effects her medication had on her behavior, but it also highlighted another aspect of the parent-child dynamics that ADHD placed on our family. My heart ached when I put myself into Sam's shoes and read the following excerpts through her eyes: *I believe that my lack of knowledge regarding exactly what ADHD was while I was growing up made it hard for me to take control of it . . . Something I was unable to understand or verbalize as a child . . . Unable to find the right words . . . Unable to defend my disability at the time.*

Her words made me regret that we didn't include her in more of the discussions about her disability, encourage her to explain how she felt when arguments erupted, take her input into consideration when making decisions, or shift some of the responsibility to her. Had we done so, we might have been able to curtail much of the negative behavior and help Sam feel more in control and part of the solution rather than the target of our frustrations and unintentional criticism.

It was too late to change the past—I knew that. Still, I resolved to keep what I'd just learned from Sam's paper in the front of my mind for future reference.

Meanwhile, Sam's first semester of her senior year was coming to an end—and imagine how excited I was when I saw "Dean's List" posted under her grades for that term! More than anything else, it was a clear indication that her self-imposed contract, with graduation as the grand prize, was working better than anything I might have come up with.

Her last semester progressed just as smoothly, and she earned the remaining credits needed without a problem. With graduation just around the corner, I was finally able to breathe a sigh of relief.

I had hoped that the last days of Sam's college experience would be less stressful than the first, but that turned out to be wishful thinking. As Barry, Dana, Grandma Carol, my sister-in-law Debbie, and I were getting ready to leave for Sam's graduation, I was full of excitement and prouder than I've ever been of her accomplishments. Prior to her arrival at our house, however, Debbie called with some disturbing news.

"Hey, Aim, I just went online to check the graduation schedule of activities, and I don't see Sam's name on the website list of graduates. Do you have any idea why?"

As she shared this unsettling discovery with us, a familiar sense of dread came over me. Trying not to assume the worst and hoping there was a mistake, I immediately hung up and called Sam to find out what the problem was.

"Sam, Aunt Debbie just called and said your name is not on the list of graduates. Do you know why that is?"

"I have no idea . . . ." She started to cry. "Mom, can you call the school to find out, please? I'm so upset because I got into a big argument with my roommate last night, and I'm trying to deal with that now! I'm sorry."

Given Sam's emotional state, I agreed to call the school to find out what was going on. But when I put down the phone and realized it was too early to call, we decided to take a leap of faith and start our journey anyway.

As we got into the car, I was nervous about the outcome—and disappointed. This was definitely not the way I wanted to start Sam's graduation weekend. I was also concerned about the calls I would be making with my mother-in-law in the car as my passenger since Barry, Dana, and Debbie were driving in his car. Although things were much better between Carol and me these days, I wasn't quite sure how she would react to this news. With butterflies in my stomach and a heavy heart, I started the ignition and hoped that we wouldn't be returning home sooner than planned.

The first hour of our ride to Sam's school was uneventful, but as it got closer to when I had planned on making the call, I began to worry. Pushing down my fear that Sam might not be graduating, and forcing myself to ignore the fact that my mother-in-law was sitting next to me, I pulled the car over and dialed the number.

"Hello, this is Samantha Kaufman's mother. I understand that her name is not on the list of graduates. Can you tell me what the problem is?"

"Sure, let me take a look. Okay, I see that the reason Sam is not on the list is that we don't have her pink name card, which is needed to identify the graduates who will be walking in the procession. Sam should have received a packet with the card in it several months ago, but it looks like she neglected to hand it in."

Wait, that's it? That has to be something we can fix! I finally let myself breathe. "It's not too late, is it?" I asked.

"Not at all, Mrs. Kaufman. Sam will be able to graduate with her class if she goes to the office and fills out the card today before five."

Phew! Still avoiding eye contact with my mother-in-law—but with a much lighter heart—I called Sam to tell her the good news. Although she was still upset about the argument with her roommate, she was able to interrupt her sobbing to tell me, "Oh, I think the packet with the pink card might be under the backseat of my car. I totally forgot about that!"

At that moment, all I could think about was the popular saying: "The more things change, the more they stay the same." It brought me back to Sam's early years in school when we would find her missing homework assignments crumpled up in the bottom of her knapsack weeks later.

Hoping that Sam would be in a better mood when we arrived and that the graduation festivities would begin with everyone smiling and celebrating her accomplishments, I said in a calm voice, "Wait for me to get there and I will go with you to fill out the card. Love you, Sammy!"

I braced myself as I hung up the phone with Sam, expecting Carol to say something negative or even just to have that look on her face that had always made me feel so judged in the past.

Instead, she reached over and touched my arm. "I'm so impressed at the way you handled this situation in such a calm and loving manner."

Surprised—and gratified—I released the tension I was holding and my whole body relaxed. "Thank you, Carol."

I smiled as I got back onto the highway and headed to my daughter's college graduation—a graduation that I'd often wondered if I would ever get to attend.

When we woke up the morning of graduation, the skies were cloudy, and rain was in the forecast, but that didn't stop us from shining our love and admiration on Sam's big day. Since we were staying in a hotel a distance from her house, I was disappointed that we weren't able to see her before the ceremony began. But that feeling quickly dissipated while we were sitting in our seats and Sam texted me to say they were starting to walk. With the excitement mounting and my heart racing, something drew me to the back of the field near the pathway of the procession. Much to my surprise, as I approached the fence, Sam and her friends were walking toward me at that exact moment. I snapped a picture as she passed by with a smile on her face and a stride in her walk that said more than words could ever express.

We sat through the program with the threatening rain overhead but never once allowed the inclement weather to interfere with our excitement and anticipation of watching Sam receive her hard-earned and well-deserved diploma. As the trials and tribulations of the past twenty-two years floated in and out of my mind, my heart filled with joy.

When they started to call the Ks, I walked to the front so I could take a picture and document this emotional moment. But when Sam walked across the stage, all I could do was stare at my baby girl in awe and wipe tears from my eyes. I was thankful that the college photographer snapped a picture, but even if he hadn't, the smile on Sam's face and the image of her hand reaching out to receive her diploma would have been engraved in my heart forever.

13

A NEW BEGINNING

WHEN SAM MOVED HOME AFTER graduation, we were looking forward to the next stage in her life. After settling in, we expected her to reach out to headhunters and join her friends in their pursuit of a paying job. Instead, Sam dragged her feet and decided to wait until September to begin her search. Obviously, this didn't sit well with Barry or me, which led to a few very contentious months. Instead of sending out resumes and going on interviews, she spent most of her time hanging at the pool in our backyard on sunny days or curling up on the couch to watch television when it was raining. We were frustrated when she disregarded our suggestions to reach out to some of our friends who might be able to help. However, when she reminded us of her success in finding her first internship in college, we backed off and let her lead the way.

When Sam finally retired her bathing suit for a business suit, she contacted headhunters and began networking with people she knew who had jobs in communications. Barry and I suggested that she contact one of our family friends in the TV industry. Once again, she rejected our idea, but this time she explained why.

"Mom, Dad, please stop," she said emphatically. "I don't want to work with someone who knows me and my background. I want to start my career with a clean slate—with people who don't know about my personal life."

Sam's explanation touched my heart and helped me feel more comfortable about taking a backseat while she navigated her own job search. Although we were concerned that finding something would be almost impossible, as it was 2008 and the whole country was in a financial crisis—Sam kept a positive attitude and persevered.

A few days after that conversation, she came running into the living room where Barry and I were sitting.

"Guess what? I just got an email from a friend of Dana's. She knew I was looking for a job and told me the company she works for is looking for an assistant media planner. Since this is exactly the type of job I'm looking for, I'm going to send her my resume right now and hopefully arrange to speak with someone in their Human Resources Department."

I was so excited for Sam—and touched that Dana had reached out to her network of friends on her sister's behalf. Our two girls had grown a lot closer over the last few years.

In college, Sam had documented her feelings about growing up with Dana in an essay she let me read: *Living in the shadow of my older sister Dana has never been easy for me because she has always held the role of the "good" child. Since Dana lived up to everyone's expectations by being smart and well-behaved, it was only natural that I was viewed as the "bad" kid because of my negative behavior, and for most of my childhood, I never hesitated to live up to my position in our family.*

After reading this, I wondered if the tension between the two of them was, in fact, sibling rivalry. But then I kept reading. In spite of the normal feelings of jealousy and resentment that Sam first wrote about, she went on to acknowledge that her negative behavior could have been precipitated by something else. *Although I was very*

argumentative and caused havoc from early on, I came to understand
that a great deal of my many tantrums were attributed to my ADHD,
which I was diagnosed with at the age of ten.

From early on, I worried about their turbulent relationship. Dana
held Sam to extremely high standards. She had trouble understanding
why her sister didn't show the same respect for Barry and me as she
did or why Sam consistently lashed out when things didn't go her way.
From Sam's point of view, I could imagine how frustrating it must
have been having an older sister who was even-tempered and well-behaved and who always strived for perfection—a sister who most people
viewed as the "perfect child." Unfortunately for Sam, being compared
to Dana highlighted her shortcomings even more and often fueled her
undesirable behavior. But none of this stopped them from ultimately
developing a loving bond and special friendship.

Dana once confided in me that she viewed her relationship with
Sam through a different lens than mine. "I know you worried about
us," she told me, "but growing up with Sam had a positive effect on
my own development in spite of the many fights and arguments we
had. I realized as I grew older that I am more understanding, patient,
and tolerant of others as a direct result of my childhood experiences
with Sam. I know I used to get really angry with her and wished she
acted differently toward me, but I never lost the love and protective
feeling I had for my baby sister from the day she was born."

Seeing how she was coming through for her sister yet again and
remembering that conversation, I had no doubt that she'd meant
every word.

A week after sending her resume, Sam called me and could barely
contain her excitement. "Mom, Mom, I got the job!! I'm starting in
two weeks. I'm sooooo excited!"

"Oh, my God, Sam, that's amazing," I exclaimed. "I'm so proud
of you! I can't wait to celebrate when you get home."

When Barry heard the news, he felt the same excitement. As Sam matured and her behavior improved, he had learned to focus on her positive growth and development that was emerging. Over time, I'd watched the friction between the two of them lessen, making room for a healthier relationship rooted in mutual love and nurtured by an abundance of humor.

We were both relieved and very proud of Sam for picking herself up off the couch and taking action. I know it wasn't easy for her since she has always had a hard time with change. However, I feel as though this major turning point in Sam's life laid a solid foundation for her future in the work world and helped build her self-confidence at the same time.

It was the night before Sam's first day of her new job, and I had just dropped her at Dana's apartment in NYC. She was going to sleep there so her morning commute would be easier. As I sat in my car driving home, I glanced over at the empty passenger seat next to me. With a lump in my throat, I reached over and touched the seat, vividly remembering the day so many years earlier when Sam sat next to me and declared, "It's not easy being me."

For the duration of the ride home, my thoughts traveled through time as I flashed back to the day my happy, content baby girl was born. With my emotions running high, I gripped the steering wheel, bracing myself for the slideshow of the next twenty-two years that rushed into my mind's eye.

My heart ached as I watched the early years of turmoil and uncertainty unfold. A cathartic feeling came over me as I forgave Sam and myself for the heated arguments that consistently tested our relationship. I continued to watch as our unwavering, unconditional love for each other remained intact throughout the difficult years leading up to her diagnosis. I marveled at my persistence and Sam's ability to persevere in spite of the mounting obstacles on the road to acceptance and seeking help. I watched her stumble at times but found myself cheering in the background as she always managed to pick herself up and move forward. I started to cry as I saw myself hesitantly cutting the cord and letting Sam go as she navigated her way through college without me. I exploded with pride watching her receive her college diploma and then, a few months later, land her first job.

As my forty-five-minute slideshow came to an end, I sat in my driveway, reflecting on my feelings and the events that brought me to that day. I thought about Sam sitting in the passenger seat just a short while ago and the conversation that had taken place. Although she was excited about her new job, Sam was also nervous and unsure of what was yet to come. She had enjoyed her four-month hiatus after graduation and worried about how she would handle her new routine and responsibilities. As we pulled up to Dana's apartment, she turned to me and jokingly said, "My life is over!"

Without hesitation, I reassured her, "No, it's not over! It's a new beginning!" At that, we both smiled and silently acknowledged this major turning point in both of our lives.

Now, as I replayed the moment when Sam got out of the car and took the first step toward the rest of her life, I was overwhelmed.

I inhaled deeply.

I exhaled slowly.

I felt twenty-two years of uncertainty melt away.

Uplifted by that feeling, I tucked the roller-coaster ride of emotions and events that brought me to that moment inside of my heart for safekeeping and opened the car door—and I, too, took the first step toward the rest of my life.

EPILOGUE

LOOKS LIKE WE MADE IT

IN THE INTRODUCTION OF MY BOOK, I wrote about the day Sam turned to me in the car and declared, "It's not easy being me." From that day forward, I held on to my wish for the future that the next time she pondered her life as we were driving in the car, she might turn to me and say, "I love being me" instead. The night when she and I drove to New York before her first day at work would have been the perfect setting for my wish to come true. But at that point, all she could think about was her new job and how nervous she was.

Sam started her job knowing that her life would change, and she worried that it might not be for the better. The first few weeks were stressful as she learned new skills, met new people, and developed a work ethic that fit her personality. I watched her insecurities melt away as she gained confidence and comfort with her surroundings and daily responsibilities. Her outlook turned a corner, and her self-esteem blossomed as her creative ideas and proposals caught the attention of her superiors and clients.

Even with the success she was having at the office, I noticed that Sam typically returned home at the end of the day in a bad mood. After reflecting on what she had written about coming down from her medication in the paper I'd read just a few months earlier, I tried a new approach with her. Instead of initiating a conversation that might lead to an argument, I asked her one evening, "Hey, Sam, you seem tired. What can I do to help?"

"You're right. I am in a bad mood, but I think it's because I'm coming down from my medicine," she said. "I'm going to get something to eat and go up to my room for a while. So, please leave me alone, and I'll come down later to tell you about my day, okay?"

I was so proud of my daughter for learning how to express her feelings and communicate her needs. "That sounds like a great plan," I said.

About an hour later, Sam came downstairs—totally agreeable and ready to talk about her day and help me cook dinner.

Keeping in mind what Sam had written in her essay and including her in the problem-solving process turned the following months into an enjoyable bonding experience for the two of us and helped solidify the foundation of our relationship into something even more unshakable than it had been before.

Just five months after beginning her new career, Sam showed me a piece of paper she was holding in her hand when she got home from work. "I got my first performance evaluation today," she announced. "Do you want me to read it to you?"

Excited to hear what it said, I replied, "Yes, of course."

"It's long, so I'll read a few of the highlights and let you read the rest." With a big smile on her face, she started. "Let's see. Okay, here: *Sam has a great personality and interacts well with co-workers; Sam takes pride in her work and consistently meets deadlines; Sam has a good work ethic and takes direction well.*"

After Sam read a few more select parts of her rave review to me, I read the rest myself, tears rolling down my cheeks. Compliments and praises of her work abilities filled the pages. I wished I could send that evaluation to every teacher, therapist, doctor, and camp director who'd ever doubted her integrity or questioned her ability to succeed. I'd always hoped that Sam would find her way and be successful at whatever career path she chose, but I'd also wondered frequently along the way how she would overcome her shaky past to get there. After reading the accolades in her review, however, all remaining doubts vanished.

As I made plans to frame this astonishing testament to Sam's accomplishments, my heart did a little dance. My younger daughter was really on her way now.

A few days after receiving her positive evaluation, Sam and I went out for dinner to celebrate. Sitting at the table, we talked about different people in our lives and discussed their various personality traits as well as our own.

Reflecting on her past, Sam confessed, "I didn't want to pass my college courses for myself. It was because I didn't want to disappoint you and Daddy. Knowing that you guys believed in my abilities gave me the motivation to succeed. The consequences you included in the contracts during my first two years of college pushed me to not only apply myself but to exceed your expectations of me!"

Hearing that the trust Barry and I had shown in her, even in the tough times, had helped build her confidence and belief in herself was the greatest compliment I could have gotten from Sam.

"Oh, Sam, I know I keep telling you this, but I am so proud of you," I said, blinking back tears. "Knowing that some of the things we did had such a positive effect on your confidence and desire to succeed is everything a parent could want to hear from their child. Thank you so much for sharing your thoughts with me. I can't wait to see where life takes you from here."

Uplifted by our heartwarming conversation, I was sure that wherever that place turned out to be, it would be magical.

∿

It was later that night, while we were sitting on the living room couch watching TV together, that Sam turned to me and said what I had been waiting to hear for so long: "Mom, I was thinking . . . there's no one else I'd rather be."

Absorbing her words, I smiled from the place deep within my heart that had long held my everlasting hope that one day Sam would once again be my happy, content baby girl. Then I acknowledged with conviction, *There's no one else I'd rather be either.*

And I meant it with all of my heart.

When the thought of writing a book first crossed my mind, I envisioned myself transcribing stories about my daughter's life through my eyes. But after sitting down at my computer, I was surprised to see that what was appearing on the screen was more about me than Sam. I often found myself revising my original outline and earlier chapters to reflect this new vision of what soon became a memoir about my experiences of raising a child with ADHD.

As the transcript of my personal journey evolved, the one constant that remained in the back of my mind, prodding me along, was the hope that one day I would completely emerge from the dark tunnel that had consumed much of my existence that started in Sam's early childhood. Throughout the process, I saw glimpses of light each time my daughter located bits of inner peace and experienced personal triumphs. Watching her graduate from high school and then college, without a doubt, brought the light much closer. But it was something that happened almost two years after her college graduation that lit up my heart completely and made me think that I had finally reached the end of the tunnel.

My mother was living with us when Sam moved home after her college graduation. Their relationship grew into something special as Sam bonded with her Grandma Glady, whom she lovingly referred to as her "roommate." I didn't realize just how special it really was until

Sam stood up to deliver her eulogy at my mother's funeral a year and a half later.

Sam stepped up to the podium, looked around the room, and then began: "One of the most meaningful lessons I learned from my grandma was to never give up and to try to look at the positive aspect of every situation. Watching her get out of bed every day with a smile on her face was truly the most inspirational thing I have ever seen."

Her voice filled with emotion as she continued, "I remember a specific week when I was having a particularly hard time at work and found myself incredibly overwhelmed to the point where I wanted to give up and quit. She didn't know this, but the person who truly helped me get through that week was my Grandma Glady. I thought about her and how much she had gone through in her life without so much as one complaint. I ended up getting through that week, and when I got home on Friday, she told me how proud she was of me. In that one moment, a funny thing happened: for the first time in my life, I felt completely and truly proud of myself."

Tears streamed down my cheeks as I listened to this heartfelt tribute to my mother. But Sam wasn't done yet.

"The last thing I would like to share with all of you is the pride I feel for my mother. Through her, I have learned what it is like to be truly selfless. Mom, the way you cared for Grandma Glady showed me an act of love beyond anything I have ever witnessed. Your ability to change your life the way you have in the past two years is truly incredible. Every day you become more and more like Grandma. I have always known what a great mother you are, but today, I want you to know that you, too, like Grandma Glady, are a great lady."

And with that, I was sobbing.

Throughout Sam's childhood, the frequency with which I was criticized for the way I was raising her often made me doubt my parenting abilities. Over time, I learned to trust my heart, rely on my maternal instincts, and refer to my invaluable research to guide me in what I hoped was the right direction—but that doesn't mean I was always able to tune out the critics, internal or external, that voiced their doubts about my approach on an ongoing basis. Although I got better at it the more progress Sam made, it wasn't until I sat down to write this chapter that I truly shed all my doubts and embraced the fact that I did right by my baby girl.

I have always known what a great mother you are. Those words echoed in my mind and came into focus within my heart as I thought back to my mother's memorial. What better validation could I ask for than to hear this affirmation directly from my daughter—the very daughter whose struggles had made me question my choices and abilities as a parent for so many years? Turning this memory over in my mind, I believed that the light I had been seeking couldn't shine any brighter.

But it was something that Sam wrote in my Mother's Day card six months later that made me realize that every decision I made, every conflict I endured, and every tear I shed was leading me to this one shining moment.

Dear Mom, thank you for always loving me.

Reading these words, I felt the troubling events of the past and any remaining doubt melt away and vacate my heart, crowding out that dark tunnel for good and making room for the brightest light I could ever have hoped for to shine through.

ABOUT THE AUTHOR

photo credit to Bill Marvin

AIMEE KAUFMAN SPENT MANY HOURS during her younger daughter's childhood learning about attention deficit hyperactivity disorder (ADHD) and advocating for her needs while working part-time as an accountant. Along the way, she discovered that she has adult ADHD, which provided her with a unique insight into her daughter's disability. Today, Aimee owns her own QuickBooks consulting business and cherishes the time she and her husband spend in Jersey City with their grown daughters (and their husbands). Aimee and her husband, Barry, live in Berkeley Heights, NJ.

Looking for your next great read?

We can help!

Visit www.shewritespress.com/next-read
or scan the QR code below for a list
of our recommended titles.

She Writes Press is an award-winning
independent publishing company founded to
serve women writers everywhere.